SOURAV GANGULY

THE LORD OF CRICKET

SOURAV GANGULY

THE LORD OF CRICKET

DEBASISH DATTA

FOREWORD
GEOFFREY BOYCOTT

NIYOGI
BOOKS

Special thanks to
AAJKAAL Publishers
MID-DAY, Mumbai

Published by
NIYOGI BOOKS
Block D, Building No. 77,
Okhla Industrial Area, Phase-I,
New Delhi-110 020, INDIA
Tel: 91-11-26816301, 26818960
Email: niyogibooks@gmail.com
Website: www.niyogibooksindia.com

Photographs by: Pradeep Mandhani, Bikash Sadhu, Santi Sen, Ronny Roy
Pradip Dutta, Sankar Nag Das, Gautam Bhattacharya,
Stefen John & from Dona Ganguly's collection

Edited by: K.E. Priyamvada
Design: Shaju K. Anthony

ISBN: 978-93-89136-35-7

Year of Publication: May 2007
Revised Edition: 2020

Printed at: Niyogi Offset Pvt. Ltd., New Delhi, India

Dedicated to
my wife Pamela Datta, my daughters
Priyadarshini, Pratyusha
and all the members of the
Sourav Ganguly fan club

Contents

Foreword

Born to lead

A few years back, when I first heard that Sourav Ganguly was making his foray into cricket administration, I must confess that I was taken by surprise. It wasn't because I didn't believe he would make a capable administrator. I felt Sourav would be more at home doing media. But the more I thought about it, the more I realised what a great development it was from a cricketing point of view.

Sourav is one of the most passionate, insightful and intelligent cricketers I have come across, and I have seen a few in my lifetime! My first interaction with him was at Lord's in 1996, when he made a sublime hundred on Test debut. He came across as knowledgeable and respectful, but also with firm conviction. That was the start of a wonderful relationship that I cherish to this date.

When Sourav got into the Cricket Association of Bengal, I sent him a congratulatory message, and told that in a few years' time, I would again congratulate him on becoming the President of the Board of Control for Cricket in India! Sure enough, when he became the BCCI head in October 2019, I reminded him of my prediction of a few years. As always, we had a good laugh about this too.

I believe it is wonderful for the sport that a former national skipper, and a successful one at that, is helming the most powerful and influential cricket board in the world. Sourav's heart is firmly in cricket, and already, he has taken several initiatives that are bound to benefit the sport and its primary stakeholders. My 'Prince of Kalkuta' will soon become the king of the cricket world, of that I have no doubt.

Mike Brearley once told me how much he had appreciated and respected Sourav's inputs during their stint together with the MCC's World Cricket Committee. Mike was one of England's more successful captains and is an acknowledged thinker of the game. His words carry a great deal of weight, though he wasn't telling me anything that I didn't know previously.

From what I am hearing, Sourav's stint as the BCCI president will end in 10 months' time because of the 'cooling off' period that has been incorporated into the updated constitution. To me, this cooling off is a load of poppycock. What we must always understand is that there can be no compromises when it comes to taking our great game forward. It is impossible for anyone to trigger a turnaround in such a short span of time, especially when you are taking charge of the association at a troubled time like Sourav has. I hope saner counsel prevails and Sourav gets a longer run as the BCCI president, because he is the right man for the job given how much he cares for cricket, and given his pedigree as a player, as a captain and as a leader.

I have the greatest admiration for Sourav the captain. I was amazed to learn that India had won only 13 Tests abroad before Sourav took over the captaincy. It is an amazing piece of statistics, which summed up the story of Indian cricket nicely until Sourav decided to take the bull by the horns. Now, under Virat Kohli, the Indians have exploded the myth that they do not travel well.

Under Sourav, India won no fewer than 11 Tests abroad. Not massive by any standards but when you consider that they had only 13 away Test victories earlier, it is a commendable achievement in five years. Now, if you think India only won in Bangladesh and Zimbabwe under Sourav, you are wrong. Sourav's first away victory was in Bangladesh and the last in Zimbabwe, but let's not forget that in between, India pulled off victories in England, West Indies, Sri Lanka, Australia and Pakistan, too. This is something no Indian team had managed previously.

Sourav had a wonderful team at his disposal and the players under him worked hard to put up a united front. The basics were adhered to and commitment was a natural ally. They were honest enough to try and change things continuously. Indian cricket needed planning, sincerity and self-belief. Fanfare is fine but cricket is serious business. It's a full-time job. One has to continually strive to improve.

I saw that zeal among the players when the Indians were led by Sourav. He was a natural leader of men, who led by instinct rather than planning on most of the occasions. And he seemed to have injected a

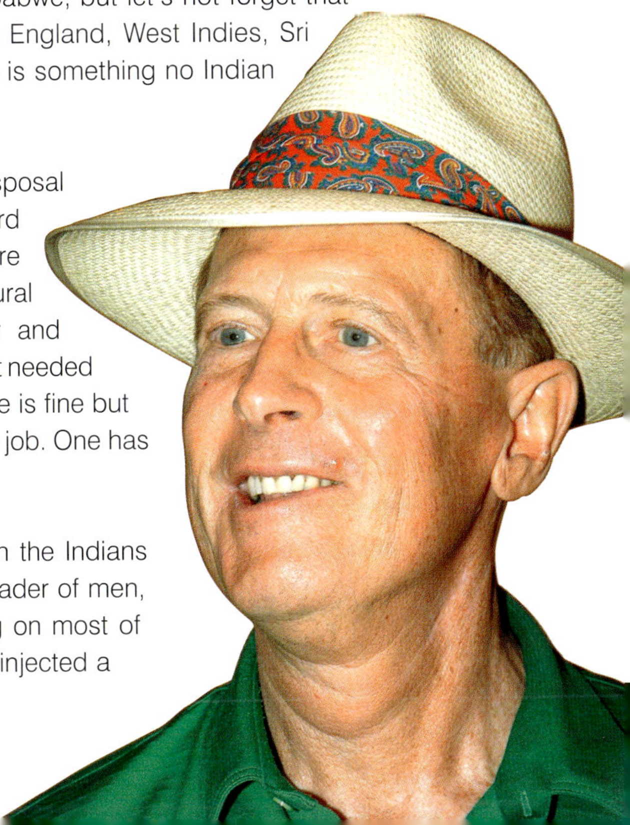

sense of pride in his players who began to believe that they could really compete with the best in business.

In all my years of playing and commentating on the game, I have never seen a better timer of the ball than Sourav Ganguly. And believe me, I have seen quite a few exquisite players. I still cannot forget his first Test hundred at Lord's. Not once did the England bowlers manage to beat him outside the off-stump.

I have known the author of this book, Debasish Datta, since my playing days. In the past decade or so, we have often exchanged notes while on tours. Most of the time we have ended up discussing two cricketers: Both with identical initials S.G. (Sunil Gavaskar and Sourav Ganguly)

I have known Sunil for a long time. He is extremely witty, articulate and a keen student of the game. Even today, he knows exactly where his off-stump is. Similarly I am very fond of Sourav. I am also aware that Debu, as I often refer to him, shares a special bond with the 'Prince of Kalkuta'.

He has followed Sourav's career very closely and is best placed to write on various facets of this very talented cricketer. Having seen Debu following the fortunes of Indian cricket, I can safely say that he is the right man to paint a portrait of India's most successful cricket captain.

His is a view from just behind the first slip. And like a good slip-catcher, Debu is not known to miss much. Here is hoping that his latest 'catch' will be as spectacular as some of his previous ones...

Best wishes to Debu and his book.

Geoffrey Boycott

Introduction

The importance of being Sourav Ganguly

The story of Sourav Ganguly is essentially that of a bright young lad's metamorphosis into a leader of men in a battlefield called cricket. It is the kind of stuff that fairy tales are made of. Among Bengalis, widely bantered as chicken-hearted, butter-fingered, soft and sentimental blokes, Sourav has been a glorious exception. His figures in the field speak for themselves. His 11,000-plus runs in the shorter version of the game also include 22 hundreds. Rarely has India lost when Sourav has scored. His 31 Man-of-the-Match awards bear testimony to the considerable influence he usually exerted on a cricket match. Along the way he has been fined, censured and suspended, but he couldn't care less, for he has always played the game on his own terms.

Perhaps the most precious Bengali icon after Rabindranath Tagore and Satyajit Ray, Sourav's exploits on the pitch have earned him name and fame that has transcended Bengali sub-nationalism and infected the entire cricket world. During his tenure as the unquestionable leader of the national cricket team, Sourav personified the world of difference that lies between style and substance. He spotted the gulf between just wanting to be part of the show and daring to push the limits. He is the man who can be credited with building Team India, brick by brick. Never before did an Indian captain look more authoritative than this inspirational Kolkatan, who betrays a lazy elegance at the crease. Like an able commander, he has always been alive to the situation in the middle and executed every plan with purpose and intent in a bid to maximise results.

Certainly, he isn't the coolest dude in town, but enormously to his credit, Sourav not only succeeded in pulling the Indian team out from the depths of despairing mediocrity (the *chalta hai* culture), but also managed to get the best out of each individual player. He taught them to look the enemy in the eye and play the game the hard way. Under Sourav, India at last became a team that refused to get overawed by the reputation of their opponents. If someone dared him, he took up the challenge. When Andrew Flintoff took off his shirt in Mumbai, Sourav replied by baring his chest on the Lord's balcony. For him, self-respect has always meant much more than sepia-tainted customs.

At times, he may have betrayed some arrogance, but all those who know him closely will tell you that despite earning both fame and fortune, Sourav remains pretty level-headed. But success didn't come to him on a platter. He had to toil for it like lesser mortals despite getting a headstart in his cricket career. When Sourav made his first-class debut in the final of the Ranji Trophy against Delhi in 1989-90, the whole of Bengal erupted in joy at having unearthed a wonderkid, who, at 16, looked ready to take on the world. Success often takes a torturous route as was the case with Souray. His maiden appearance for the state team didn't yield many runs, certainly not enough to win him a national call-up.

His next big opportunity finally arrived when he was picked for the 1991-92 tri-series Down Under. But hope soon gave way to despair when he was cast aside after failing on his ODI debut. A chastened Sourav returned to domestic cricket and started rebuilding his career all over again. After spending four years in near-oblivion, Sourav made the cut for India's tour of England in 1996, thanks to East Zone selector Sambaran Banerjee's powers of persuasion, who made sure that the Bengal youngster was chosen as 'a fifth-pacer, who could also bat'. Not many people were happy with such a controversial selection, but it hardly mattered to Sourav, who simply waited for the next opportunity to come his way. It wouldn't have come had not his room-partner on the tour, the headstrong Navjot Sidhu staged an unprecedented walk-out from the team following differences with captain Mohammed Azharuddin.

The 'fifth-pacer' was asked to make his Test debut at Lord's, but as a No. 3 batsman after India had lost the opening Test rather tamely. Undaunted by the enormity of the occasion, Sourav prepared himself for the task on hand. It was while he was practising at Lord's that English legend Geoffrey Boycott first noticed Sourav, whom he later re-christened as 'The Prince of Kolkata'. And by his own admission, Boycott fell in love with Sourav's elegant left-handed strokeplay. 'There was something in his face that had caught my attention. Later, I simply fell in love with his batting,' Boycott says of his first impressions about Sourav. 'When in full flow, there is no better timer of the ball than Sourav,' he has acknowledged. Fittingly enough, Lord's was the venue of the rebirth of a man, who was destined to rule his country's cricket. A century on his debut characterised his innate grit and flamboyance. The BBC picked him as their Man of the Match. Boycott, too, doffed his hat. Richie Benaud sported a sweet smile. The Bengalis danced on the streets with unbounded joy and the country rejoiced.

If there were still any critics and doubters, they were silenced once and for all by Sourav who notched up a second successive Test century at Trent Bridge. And the 'fifth-pacer' also took vital wickets to earn the Man-of-the-Match award. A hero was born. The Bengalis had found an icon. Tribulation had given way to triumph. When he returned to

Kolkata, thousands of Kolkatans lined up on both sides of the street from the Taratala intersection on Diamond Harbour Road to his Biren Roy Road residence near Behala Chowrasta. Sourav had good reason to believe that he had exorcised the ghost of the past (1992-96) with his super show in England. Sourav was now hot property. Coach Sandeep Patil burnt his hands when he dumped him for a match in the 1996 Sahara Cup. Patil ultimately lost his job. In the next edition of the Sahara Cup at Toronto, Sourav won four MoM awards in five matches, taking wickets and scoring runs almost at will. His all-round versatility fetched him the Man-of-the-Series award as well as a brand new Opel Astra car, that served him for long.

Till now, considered to be a good Test match player, Sourav, realising the need of the hour, gradually changed his game and turned himself into an opener in ODIs. And with Sachin Tendulkar, he formed one of the most potent opening pairs in one-day cricket. It was perhaps one of the most successful journeys in togetherness in Indian cricket. Sachin and Sourav scripted some memorable opening partnerships, including a world record stand of 252 versus Sri Lanka. In the 1999 World Cup, Sourav teamed up with Rahul Dravid to set another world record—adding 318 runs for the second wicket against Sri Lanka to add another feather to his cap. In doing so, Sourav registered his highest individual score (183 not out versus Sri Lanka).

And when Sachin stepped down from the captaincy for a second time in 2000, it was time for Maharaja to assume the throne of Indian cricket. Displaying unmatched tenacity and great statesmanship, Sourav led India's charge towards a new horizon.

With coach John Wright, Sourav forged a highly successful partnership and helped groom a number of youngsters, including Virender Sehwag, Yuvraj Singh and Harbhajan Singh. Despite their early failures and inconsistency, Sourav backed them to the hilt and fought with the Indian Cricket Board and the selectors to keep them in the squad. To their credit, all three subsequently won matches for India and went on to become core components of Team India. Steve Waugh and his all-conquering band of Australians were given a taste of their own medicine by Sourav and his boys. Australian cricketers, who had, over the years, mastered the art of sledging, were paid back in the same coin by a bunch of new and brash Indian kids, led by Sourav. The message to Waugh went out loud and clear when he was kept waiting by the Indian captain for the toss. Not used to being bullied by others, Australians looked rattled and ended up losing the 2001 Test series in India 1-2. Harbhajan Singh and VVS Laxman may have been the architects of India's historic win at the Eden Gardens, but 'Dada's *dadagiri*' had played no mean role in that series equalling win. And when the spirited Indians scripted another fairy tale win in Chennai to clinch the rubber, the Aussies went home a dejected lot having failed to conquer the 'Final Frontier'. Sourav himself led India's World Cup campaign in 2003, and though India lost to Australia in the final in South Africa, it was another high-point of his career. It was at this stage that Sourav's form began to falter. Not the one to sweat over it, Sourav sought professional advice and got it from the best. He travelled to Australia where Greg Chappell helped him iron out minor flaws in his game and Sourav rebounded with a splendid 144 against Australia when India toured Down Under later that year. That innings in Brisbane ranks among his best and it helped set the tone of the series that India drew 1-1 with Waugh's men. History was created in Pakistan when India won both, the Test as well as the ODI series under Sourav. A new dawn was heralded as the Team India caravan began its journey.

Such was his stock in Indian cricket that he became a brand, and corporate houses fell over themselves to sign him up to promote their products. In Kolkata he opened a multi-cuisine restaurant—Sourav's, The Food Pavilion which has since carved a niche for itself on the city's food map. A devoted son, a caring husband and a doting father, Sourav Ganguly is a complete package. Born to Chandi and Nirupa Ganguly, Sourav and his elder brother Snehasish still live in their ancestral house in Behala under the same roof with their wives and children.

Sourav is married to his childhood sweetheart Dona, the daughter of his father's former business partner, Sanjib Roy. A noted exponent of the Odissi dance form, Dona, has stood by Sourav through thick and thin. The couple were blessed with a daughter in 2001. Sana is dad Sourav's favourite, just as he is a favourite with the masses in his home state. The near-hysteria that erupted in the country after Sourav was dropped from the Indian team merely reflected the love and affection that his countrymen have for him. To his credit, Sourav maintained a dignified silence.

By doing so, he has shown that he is man enough to absorb body-blows—some even below the belt. Yet, he remained focused in his endeavour to win back his place in the Indian team, for he believed he still had a lot to offer to the team, he had built.

His opportunities came during the South Africa tour in 2006-end and during the West Indies tour to India in early January, 2007. He grabbed these and proved to the world that with a bat in his hands, he was still worth a wager. For, there hasn't been a tougher guy in the history of Indian cricket. That he is tough as a nail, even Greg Chappell would admit. No one can take that away from him. Some love him, some love to hate him, but no one can simply ignore Sourav Ganguly.

Of sibling rivalry and bittersweet debut

Above:
The Dada with his Dada

Facing page:
Daddy cool: Sourav and father Chandi Ganguly

'Hello! This is Bobby Simpson speaking. Can I speak to Mark?'

'No, he is not here. I'm Steve.'

'Well, Steve I have bad some news for you.'

'What's that?'

'Well, you have been dropped from the Australian Test team.'

'Oh, my God!'

'However, Mark has been selected. I wanted to congratulate him.'

'That's definitely good news. But whom did he replace?'

'Sorry son, but he replaced you!'

The above lines are a transcription of a phone call Bobby Simpson, the former Australian captain and coach, had made to the Waughs on that fateful day when Mark earned his first call-up to the Australian Test squad at the expense of his twin brother Steve, who is older to him by a mere four minutes.

At night, when Mark returned home, he found his brother Steve had got over the initial disappointment at being dropped and looked determined to stage a comeback. 'Never mind Mate, we shall be playing together for Australia soon. And this time both of us will be in the squad for good,' Steve told Mark whose joy at being selected was tinged with sorrow.

Sibling rivalries are pretty common in the world of sport, especially when you have two talented sportspersons in the family.

Right:
'Congratulations' Snehasish says with a garland after Sourav came back from England in 1996

For Sourav Ganguly, his elder brother Snehasish has always been someone whom he loved, respected and looked up to. But much like the Waughs, in a bizarre twist of fate, Sourav made his first-class cricket debut replacing his 'dadabhai' (elder brother) in the 1989-90 Ranji Trophy final—easily the most important match—in the domestic cricket calendar.

It was a great setback for Snehasish, who at that stage was fighting for a place in the national team. So impressive had been the left-hander's performance earlier in the season—in the Irani Trophy as well as the Ranji Trophy—that the chairman of the Indian selection committee, Raj Singh Dungarpur had flown down to Kolkata to watch Raj (Snehasish's nickname) in action. Imagine his shock when he found Snehasish's name missing from the Bengal playing XI!

Facing page:
Daddy and his darlings at their playground called the Eden Gardens

Right:
Brotherhood of men: Sourav and Snehasish

Raj Singh later met Snehasish to explain the selectors' position. 'Look son, if you are not picked by your state to play the most important match in domestic cricket, how do you

'Well bowled!' Ajit Agarkar congratulates Sourav, the bowler

expect the national selectors to pick you for the Indian team?' Raj Singh had asked Snehasish.

It was a bitter pill for Snehasish to swallow. On one hand he was deeply disappointed at having been left out, but on the other he was very pleased for his kid brother who had taken his place in the team and desperately wanted Sourav to succeed on his debut.

It was a day of mixed feelings at the 2/6 Biren Roy Road (East) residence of the Ganguly clan. The entire locality in Barisha, a suburb in south Kolkata appeared to be affected by this bittersweet pill presented to them by the Bengal selectors.

Father Chandi Ganguly, too, was understandably tense. However, to his credit, the senior Ganguly played his part perfectly—that of a father of two immensely gifted cricketers aspiring to don India colours.

One moment he was cheering Maharaja in his room, trying to give his younger son the confidence he needed before facing such a big test. 'Look son, this is your best chance to catch the attention of everyone and you have to grab it with both hands,' he told Sourav.

'If I have an opinion, I will give it'
—with Tony Greg

In the other room, his dejected elder son, too needed his fatherly advice. 'Your turn will come again. They just cannot suppress your talent. Don't lose heart. You will definitely bounce back,' he told Snehasish in a bid to cheer him up.

To this day Snehasish believes that he shouldn't have been dropped for that match. 'I was in fine nick and had played in all the matches for Bengal in their Ranji campaign. I had also played for the Rest of India team in the Irani Trophy. I didn't deserve this,' he says with a shake of his head.

But there was hardly anything the Gangulys could do. They simply could not be very vocal about the injustice meted out to Snehasish by the Bengal selectors because it would have scarred Sourav's impressionable mind and rendered him heartbroken.

Two to Tango: with Sachin Tendulkar during Sourav's English Summer in 1996. To their right is Chris Lewis

Bengal captain Sambaran Banerjee took the cue from the Bengal selectors and decided to throw teenager Sourav into the deep end of the pool in the Ranji final. Sambaran, simply told the teenager to go out and play his natural game. It was a momentous occasion for Bengal cricket. The team needed an extra bowler against a formidable Delhi batting line-up that boasted of players like Bhaskar Pillay, Ajay Sharma and Raman Lamba—all great accumulators of runs in domestic cricket—besides maestro Mohinder Amarnath.

History would have it that Sourav had an average debut. But during his brief innings of 22 off 23 deliveries he gave enough indication of things to come. The knowledgeable and cricket loving people of Bengal had seen glimpses of pure beauty as the youngster pierced the field with flawless technique. Sourav's innings was not about the runs he scored, rather it was all about how he made them. Sourav's off-side play reminded them of a certain blond England captain (David Gower) whose left-handed elegance they had watched in awe at the Eden Gardens few years back. Sourav also got a chance to bowl, and during his six-over spell, he conceded just 19 runs.

Historic moment: Sachin reaches his 35th century. Sourav was the first to congratulate him

Importantly for Bengal and Sourav, the Ranji Trophy was won after 51 long years. Snehasish set aside his personal disappointment and rejoiced with his kid brother Sourav, who had made a winning start to his first-class career. Soon after the Ranji final was the Wills Trophy and Sourav played with such authority in that tournament that veteran player Arun Lal marked him out as a future star of Indian cricket.

The Gangulys were elated and the festivities that day at their Behala residence reminded people close to the family of the day when 'Maharaja' was born.

It may be pure coincidence that Sourav shares his birthday (July 8) with Jyoti Basu, Bengal's legendary, long-time reigning Marxist leader, but so bullish was the entire Ganguly clan about the latest addition to their family that they named him 'Maharaja' (king). It was pretty evident from an early age that Sourav was cut out for greatness. Being the youngest in the family has its advantages as well as its disadvantages, but Sourav enjoyed the best of both worlds.

His grandfather Nirad Kanta Ganguly, the patriarch of the family, doted on both Raj and Maharaja. A towering personality and a visionary, Sourav's grandfather is considered to be a pioneer in the printing business in Bengal. He set up Calcutta's most ultra-modern printing facility—NC Gossain Press—along with a friend and a partner who also lived next door.

Yuvraj and Parthiv are sombre, but their leader is not

Nirad Kanta's son Chandi played cricket for Aryan Club, but could not realise his dream of playing for Bengal. So when his sons were born, Chandi tried to make sure that they measured up to the demands of first-class cricket.

Chandi himself got into cricket administration at the club and state levels and went on to become Secretary of the Cricket Association of Bengal (CAB).

His other love—
at the
Salt Lake Stadium

Snehasish and Sourav's initiation into the game was therefore rather smooth, even though the latter had shown early promise as a footballer. An early riser himself, Chandi made sure that his beloved sons too made an early start to their day instead of remaining in bed for a few hours more. Family members say, Chandi used to pour a bucketful of water on their beds and switch off the fans if the kids refused to get up.

He would then make sure that they went straight to the gymnasium before heading for their morning cricket practice session. Sourav's mother, Nirupa, is a simple, religious and god-fearing lady. She would make sure that her sons never left the house without offering their prayers at the family prayer room (the Chandi mandap or the place where the goddess Chandi is worshipped).

Snehasish studied at South Point, while Sourav has always been a Xaverian. Nirupa never objected to her sons playing cricket or going for training sessions, but made sure that her sons never skipped school and learnt their lessons. It was, therefore, no surprise that Sourav scored 75 per cent marks in Class X and XII and went on to graduate in commerce with flying colours before cricket overtook him.

'Mom was very strict. We did have a fair bit of freedom, but there was just no way we could have skipped our lessons. Those days we used to get our weekly report cards on Mondays. We had to get them signed by one of the parents and submit it on Wednesdays. As Dad used to be very busy those days, Mom was the one who would usually put her initials. And we knew that she would not spare us if our weekly report cards didn't reflect the marks she had expected. So, we had to study hard', Sourav recollects even now.

But then, those were the early days when the younger brother was addicted to a different ball game—football. Sourav simply loved the challenge to dribble past a defender and put the ball in the net. The entire Ganguly clan also used to be very bullish about football. On the Viswakarma Puja day the Gangulys used to play a festival football match among themselves with father Chandi and uncles on one side and Sourav, Snehasish and their cousins on the other.

These annual 'numbers' used to be pretty competitive. On the ground the opponents had to be beaten. Bruised feet and egos were the order of the day as the 'young turks' charged at the 'old brigade'. Snehasish was always game for a hard tackle and was usually well supported by his younger brother.

The Eden Gardens is Sourav's home ground and he has played much of his cricket here. By his own admission, he first visited the Eden Gardens at the age of five with his father and elder brother. He still remembers that misty morning when he stood on the green lawn in front of the two dressing rooms with his brother and gazed in awe at the magnificence of the morning in the gigantic stadium.

It was love at first sight, for that memory is still etched in Sourav's mind. 'I did not know then that one day I would play for India on this very ground, but the whole ambience of the Eden Gardens was so soothing that it moved me from within,' Sourav says.

Post 1996, the Lord's became his second home after he scored a historic Test century on debut there. Since then Sourav has gone on to scale new peaks of success all over the cricketing world, including scoring a century against Pakistan on 1 December 2007 at the Eden Gardens, which is also his spiritual home.

An elated Sourav after claiming another vicitim

SANSUI
SANSUI

The fifth-pacer could bat a bit

Captions, present and future—with Mohammed Azharuddin (left) and Wasim Akram (right)

Facing page:
A renowned Xaverian

BANG! The sound of the banquet hall door closing reverberated through the corridors of New Delhi's Taj Palace on April 25, 1996. Out of the hall came Mohammed Azharuddin. The Indian captain looked very agitated and visibly angry. He gave the impression that he had just swallowed a bee. A bee from Bengal, that is. A bee called Sourav Ganguly had just been forced down his throat by the selectors. He was now saddled with a player from Bengal on the tour of England!

And just because the selector from the East Zone had put forth all kinds of weird logic. Yes, it was the same former Bengal Ranji Trophy-winning captain, instrumental in handing Sourav his first-class debut in that memorable final in 1989-90, who had just pulled off another coup. Sambaran Banerjee had always

Above left:
Sourav in traditional Bengali attire

Above:
At home with himself and his laurels

been very confident about Sourav's cricketing abilities. And he employed the same tactics he had used to include Sourav in that Ranji final in place of his elder brother Snehasish.

In the selection meeting, Sambaran highlighted Sourav's bowling abilities. He knew, in damp English conditions, Sourav's ability to swing the ball would come in handy. As India needed an all-rounder at No. 6, Sambaran's ploy worked well.

In fact, it was a master-stroke. The other selectors, along with the skipper and coach Sandeep Patil, wanted Sunil Joshi in that role. Sambaran vehemently opposed the idea. He reasoned that Joshi was basically a spinner who could bat a bit, while the team needed a batsman who could bowl a bit. In his opinion, Sourav was a far better candidate for the No. 6 slot and wanted Joshi to be picked purely as a left-arm spinner. Sambaran, of course, had come well prepared to push for Sourav's inclusion. He had jotted down each and every score of the Bengal left hander in the last three years.

He had reached Delhi two days before the selection meeting to have informal chats with Anshuman Gaekwad and Gundappa Vishwanath in a bid to convince them that adverse media

Mike Atherton's dismay is Sourav's delight, at Lords in 1996

reports about Sourav's attitude were inaccurate and misleading. Vishwanath was convinced. Patil and Azhar were not.

Azhar was the skipper during the 1992 series in Australia where Sourav's attitude was called into question. Of course, they didn't know how hard Sourav had worked after that fateful tour and how he had prepared himself for a return to international cricket in those four bleak years. So, even though both the captain and the coach were unhappy, Viswanath, the chairman of the selectors, personally guaranteed that Sourav would not create any problem on the tour.

Ultimately, he got the nod when Gaekwad too voted for him. As if on the cue, Sourav scored a century in a Deodhar Trophy game at the Wankhede Stadium during the course of which he hit some of the balls out of the ground. Ravi Shastri, in particular, praised Sourav's innings. And having played such a grand knock in Mumbai, the Mecca, of Indian cricket, the accolades kept pouring in.

It gave Sourav's career the much-needed impetus. Ever since his inglorious return from Down Under in 1992, where he played just one match, stories about his lack of guts and gumption abounded in the media, which hurt Sourav's cause. Later on in his career, we have seen Sourav carrying drinks, sharing lighter moments with his junior colleagues, but between 1992 and 1996, he suffered so many setbacks that it appeared Sourav would be lost to Indian cricket forever. During that tour of Down Under, Sourav got the opportunity to play only four matches of which three were friendlies and a lone one-day international.

He scored only three against the West Indies in that ODI before being sent back to India before the World Cup. How he got the chance to play his first one-day international, is a tale in itself.

Sourav was throwing a few balls to Krishnamachari Srikkanth, who was keen to get a feel of the ball hitting the bat, before going in to bat. Ravi Shastri had been ill. Although the team management knew about Shastri's illness, no apparent thought was given towards choosing his replacement. Five minutes before the start of the match, Sourav was informed by the team management that he would be making his ODI debut against the West Indies at Brisbane.

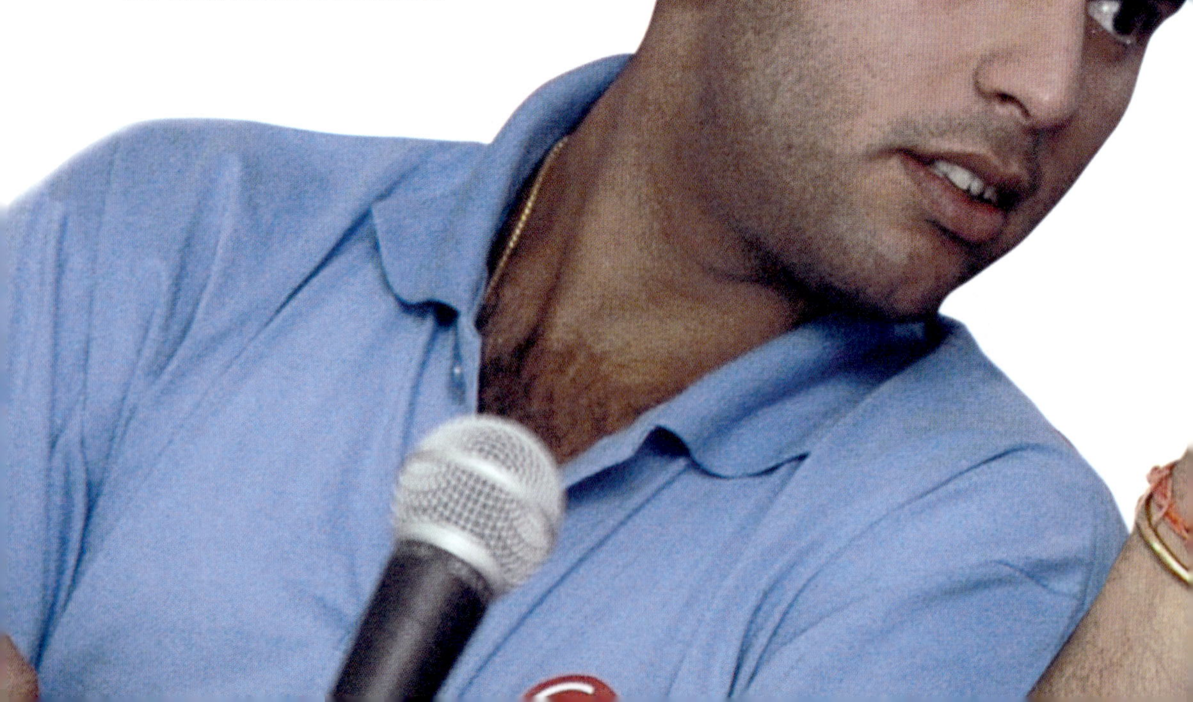

Yuvraj Singh turns to a thoughtful Sourav

Sourav, therefore, had no opportunity to prepare himself mentally for the big occasion. And the opportunity had come at the fag end of the tour when he was already a frustrated young man who had spent over a month cooling his heels inside the dressing room. The odds were loaded against him and it came as no surprise when he was adjudged lbw to Anderson Cummins after making just three. That was enough for the Indian selectors not to pick him again over the next four years!

Sourav returned dejected from Australia. He knew how it all went against him and began his preparations alone. But he was not ready to give up. He began his fight to re-establish himself, but hardly got an opportunity. He tried hard to get back into the national team on the strength of his performances in domestic cricket.

Mohinder Amarnath explains the finer points of feet movement

Every time an Indian team was selected those days, there would invariably be the usual will-he, won't-he game played in the media, which would then be quickly forgotten. Perhaps that's why when he became the captain, he tried his best to ensure that every player got at least a certain number of chances before being discarded by the selectors.

Those four years in the wilderness taught him how a young cricketer's career could be ruined and his confidence shattered if not given enough chances to succeed. Had he not backed Yuvraj and Kaif on so many occasions in the past, the selectors would have surely dropped these two talented guys and they would have been lost to Indian cricket forever.

The current Indian team is simply reaping the dividends from the investments Sourav had made into the youth few years ago when he was skipper of the side. It's precisely for these reasons that Sourav went on to be regarded as one of the top leaders in the game. All his life, Sourav has been a very straightforward person who always spoke his mind and never fired from someone else's shoulder. Even in those days, he used to maintain that he was a far better batsman than Vinod Kambli, the left-hander from Mumbai. The so-called experts used to laugh at Sourav's tall claims, for Kambli was a happening thing in Indian cricket those days. But now, after long 12-13 years, it can be said quite unequivocally that Sourav Ganguly is the best left-handed batsman India has ever produced, both in Tests as well as ODIs. Only, Sourav had to prove it the hard way.

SAH

The Lord of Lord's

NIKE

With Sandeep Patil when he was Kenya's coach, during the 2003 World Cup in South Africa

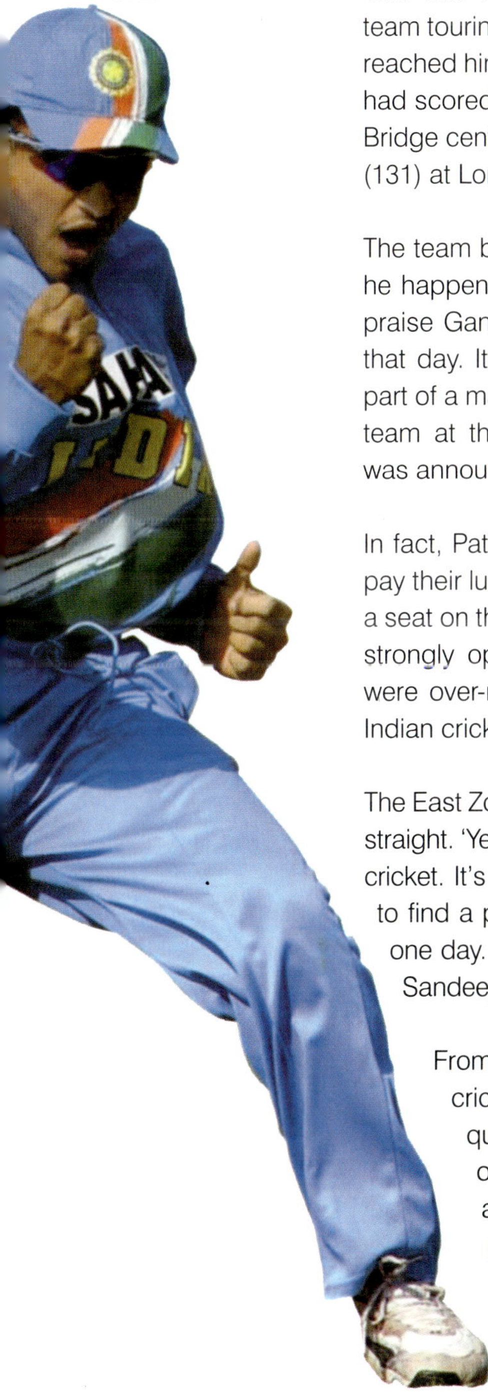

'Sourav is here, definitely, but first tell me whether the Howrah Bridge has already been named after him?'

This was how Sandeep Patil, the coach of the Indian cricket team touring England in the summer of 1996 had reacted when I reached him over telephone in Trent Bridge not long after Sourav had scored his second successive Test century (136). The Trent Bridge century, which came only a few days after his historic ton (131) at Lord's had set Indian cricket buzzing with excitement.

The team bus just left the ground, but Patil was still around and he happened to take my call. To be fair to Patil, the coach did praise Ganguly for the brilliant manner in which he had batted that day. It was certainly a pleasant change in attitude on the part of a man who had not taken Sourav's inclusion in the Indian team at the expense of Vinod Kambli well, when the squad was announced.

In fact, Patil had made East Zone selector Sambaran Banerjee pay their lunch bill as the latter had succeeded in getting Sourav a seat on the flight to England. Patil and skipper Azharuddin had strongly opposed Sourav's inclusion in the touring party, but were over-ruled by the selection committee headed by former Indian cricketer Gundappa Viswanath.

The East Zone selector had agreed readily, but also set the record straight. 'Yes, I will happily pay the bill, for it's a great day for Indian cricket. It's a matter of great pleasure for me to have been able to find a place for a cricketer who will make the country proud one day. I will pay for the lunch on that count and not for what Sandeep has just contended,' Sambaran had said.

From the very beginning, though, Sourav was labelled as a cricketer who made it to the Indian team because of the quota system in our selection process and not because of his undoubted talent with the bat and the ball. It was a stigma that Sourav needed to wipe out first. The pressure on him was choking. But what a reply he scripted with the willow at Lord's!

Above left:
Determination writ large on Sourav's face after reaching a landmark

Above:
With his Bengal mates

Ironically, his wonderful debut hundred was not enough to fetch him the Man-of-the-Match Award. The official adjudicators chose England wicketkeeper Jack Russell for his hundred in the first innings. Russell's choice caused quite a few raised eyebrows and must have broken Sourav's heart, who surely missed a well-deserved recognition. But there was good news in store for Sourav, whose morale was boosted when former England medium pacer Jonathan Agnew, representing the British Broadcasting Corporation, handed over a bottle of champagne—the Brian Johnston Award—to him as the BBC felt that he deserved the award more than anybody else. No sooner had the BBC announced its choice, than the official adjudicators were looking for a place to hide. Thankfully, the recognition for Sourav this time had come from the BBC, whose representative Agnew is a respected cricket analyst and not Sambaran Banerjee, who drew much flak in the Indian media for influencing Sourav's inclusion in the tour party.

It was a splendid innings under extreme pressure. And mind you, the English bowlers did not exactly bowl lollipops to Sourav as a large section of the Indian media would have us believe. Most of the Indian reporters on tour, reacted to Sourav's hundred with

The off-side god at work

such disdain as if he owed his feat to the English bowlers. There seemed to be a hate-Sourav campaign on in the Indian media. So no matter what he did with the bat, or ball, mattered little. They found faults with him.

The hate-Sourav campaign also spread to the English media, which gleefully picked up juicy information from Indian scribes to run down the left-hander. One Indian TV commentator consistently kept referring to Sourav as a quota-player, which was indeed very unfortunate. Sourav fans can never forget that during his debut Test match at Lord's, each boundary struck by him was followed by a typical smirk from this commentator: 'Another one? I know, another round of fireworks must have gone off in Kolkata!' It was as if Sourav were representing Kolkata, not India against England! Everybody was irked by the anti-Sourav stand of this commentator. It was absolutely uncalled for. And he continued in the same vein till Sourav cemented his place in the Indian team. Later on, of course, this commentator as well as quite a few other journalists, changed their stance and became close to him. Some even claimed to have become his friends. The same people who had maligned him for no reason when he was struggling to make his mark, had now turned his well-wishers.

SAHARA

Facing page:
Looking at the possibilities

Aren't TV professionals expected to do their homework on the game and the players before taking their place behind the microphone? Years later, the same TV channel offered Sourav a contract to join them as one of their brand ambassadors.

Earlier, the same TV channel had sponsored a Durga Puja pandal in Sourav's very own *para* (locality) which organises Durga Puja at Biren Roy Road. When reminded about those difficult times, Sourav's almost non-nonchalant. 'I have forgotten all those incidents. It is past. Life is like that,' he says.

> He may forgive and forget, but his fans find a lot of similarities between him and world renowned pole-vaulter Sergei Bubka. Like Bubka, Sourav has always bounced back whenever he has been written off.

Not many people stood by Sourav in the initial phase of his career which was rather turbulent. Among those who did, was Mumbai maestro Sunil Manohar Gavaskar. The original 'Little Master' of Indian cricket did whatever he could for the budding star. Before the tour of England, Gavaskar had requested Slazenger to sponsor Sourav's bat. And after his Lord's hundred, again on Gavaskar's request, Slazenger officials agreed to raise the sponsorship amount. They also presented Sourav with 10 new bats.

Back-to-back Test hundreds—at Lord's and Trent Bridge—also earned Sourav the Man-of-the-Series Award. This he shared with England's Nasser Hussain, who had been very consistent with the bat, too. But Sourav's achievement was even more creditable simply because he was not picked for the first Test of the three-match series. The best thing about Sourav on that tour was that he remained positive and hungry for success despite being aware of the fact that opportunities for him would be few and far between.

When one scribe asked him about his chances of breaking into the first XI, he had remarked, 'I think, I will get a chance to play a few matches. It is a long tour and they cannot deny me the opportunities. And if I get one, this time I will make it count.' He did exactly that by scoring back-to-back Test hundreds. Even in

the second innings at Trent Bridge, Sourav's bat had yielded 48 runs. So happy was his captain with his ton that he (Azharuddin) presented him with his wristwatch. Later Azhar confessed, 'None of us could judge him properly in the initial phase. A guy who has scored 10,000 ODI runs and 5,000-plus Test runs can't be an ordinary cricketer.'

It was a very honest confession from a person who clearly does not have double standards. Azhar's watch presentation was a moving gesture and it touched Sourav's heart. That wristwatch is still one of Sourav's most prized possessions and enjoys pride of place at his Behala residence in south Kolkata.

There is always a bit of history behind the creation of history and in Sourav's case it was no different. But for an extraordinary incident, Sourav wouldn't have got the chance he was so desperately craving for. Forty-six years after Lala Amarnath was controversially sent back from England by the tour management, Navjyot Singh Sidhu staged a walk-out from the squad, unable to put up with the diktats of the coach and captain. Thanks to the wonderful administrative skills of the then BCCI president Inderjit Singh Bindra who also heads the Punjab Cricket Association (PCA), one of the hottest controversies in Indian cricket was capped very nicely. But Sidhu's walk-out left a huge gap at the top of the order which needed to be filled by the team management in a hurry. They had little choice but to draft Sourav in at Lord's. What else does a captain do under such circumstances?

Azhar decided to thrust the youngster in at No. 3. Azhar, who was also the captain in 1992 on the Australia tour where Sourav had made his ODI debut, always had reservations about Ganguly and had made it pretty clear at the selection committee meeting prior to the tour of England.

Azhar, therefore, had no qualms about sending in Sourav at No. 3 after promoting Nayan Mongia to open the innings. Azhar, of course, maintains that his decision was prompted by the fact that Sourav had made runs against Derbyshire on a green-top prior to the Lord's Test.

All the same, it gave Sourav the opportunity he had been craving for. He made his debut at Lord's, considered to be the Mecca of cricket. And as far as going in at No. 3 was concerned, Sourav was not unduly worried about it even though he was not used to batting for Bengal in that position.

The new ball moves around a lot in English conditions and England bowlers are known to make the ball talk. Sourav was asked to combat the demon of seam and swing in his very first Test. He did in style and silenced his critics. What started was a sequence

Another one through extra-cover

of wonderful scores. The southpaw had scores of 131, 136 & 48, 66 & 21 not out, 6 & 0, 39 & 41, 16 & 0, 23 & 30 in his first seven Tests—a total of 557 runs at an average of 46.42, with two hundreds. His reward? A quick demotion to No. 5 in the batting order!

A Javagal Srinath straight drive in the nets had hit Sourav on his foot, forcing him out of the action for a couple of games. When he returned he found the No. 3 spot was gone. No explanations were forthcoming. None were given. But then, that's Indian cricket for you.

It was, however, given to understand that Sourav's game was not suited for the No. 3 slot. So, he was demoted to 5. Never mind. Sourav simply kept up the good work as the following scores in the next 10 Tests suggest. He had scores of 42, 6, 22 & 8, 0, 147, 109 & 45, 99, 173 & 11. In 11 innings, he made 662 runs at an average of 60.18, including three hundreds and a 99. And these runs were scored either when the team was in a good position or

FILA

Facing page:
Face-off with Ricky Ponting before the World Cup final, 2003

grafted in the company of tail-enders. After all No. 5 or 6 is hardly a position for a top-notch batsman in top form. Yet, his talent was not wasted.

It was therefore clear to Sourav from those early days that he could not take anything for granted. He was clearly not the blue-eyed boy of the team management. In his long career to follow, during which he scaled new peaks, this uncertainty always haunted Sourav. He paid the ultimate price when in 2005 he became the first Indian captain to be sacked after having won a series abroad—in Zimbabwe. Prior to Sourav's sacking only Krishnamachari Srikkanth had lost the captaincy in 1989-90 after having come back from Pakistan having drawn all five Test matches there. Also, before Sourav, no other Indian captain had even won a Test series in Zimbabwe. Not Azharuddin. Not even Sachin Tendulkar. But when Sourav came back victorious, it was merely stated that winning against Zimbabwe was no big deal. Even his painstaking hundred was dismissed as an aberration of sorts. So, he lost his captaincy as well as his place in the team! That's Indian cricket for you!

The Sachin–Sourav *jugalbandi*

Sharing a private joke with Sachin

'I know you people love me. And what you are doing now, after I have been dropped from the team, is out of love for me. But my appeal to you is to behave normally. If you continue to do it like this, it will harm our team spirit. Please remember that we are here to play for the country and are fighting against all odds. This is the right moment to back the Indian team. If you do so, it will ultimately help me, too.'

This was a brief statement issued by Sourav Ganguly to pacify his agitated fans in Kolkata after he was dropped from the first XI by the team management in Toronto 1996-97. Sourav's omission from the team during the Sahara Cup against Pakistan had sparked widespread protests in Kolkata, Sourav's home town. The Kolkatans, of course, have always reacted this way whenever they have felt that injustice has been meted out to their icons by those in authority.

So when Sourav was benched by the team management, even Sachin Tendulkar, who is otherwise quite a favourite among the sports-loving people of Kolkata, was not spared.

Incidentally, Sachin was leading the side then. And Sourav was dropped because coach Sandeep Patil wanted to play Vinod Kambli. And to justify his selection Patil kept on telling the media that Sourav was a misfit in the one-day squad.

In Sri Lanka, Sourav was asked to bat at No. 7 in a one-dayer. It was told to the media that the team management wanted someone at No. 7 who could accelerate the scoring rate if required or anchor the innings. Not one to crib about all this, Sourav made a splendid 56 in the company of Sunil Joshi. So, Sourav could not be dropped immediately.

As a senior pro, Wookeri Raman, humours Sachin and Sourav.

SAHA
SAH

At the Man-of-the Match award function. Also seen in the picture are members of the Sri Lanka team

Facing page: Another one bites the dust. Boy!

When the team reached Toronto, after Sourav had failed in the first match, Patil wielded the axe and kept him out of the second game. Sourav's substitute did nothing to justify his inclusion and after spending two matches on the bench, the 'Bengal Tiger' was back in the playing XI for the fourth match. Kolkata fans can be quite unforgiving and there were demonstrations everywhere against the team management for playing politics with Sourav. They were pacified only after Sourav got his place back in the squad.

However, when the team management came to know about the reaction of people in Kolkata, they were quite upset. 'What we are doing is for the benefit of the team. If Kolkatans do not want to realise that, they have every right to show their disappointment. But not in such a way that it affects the team spirit,' Sachin was quoted as saying.

The Tiger and the Lion

Sourav, too was worried. He had nothing to do with what was happening in Kolkata. But it appeared to the team management that Sourav was behind all this. Sourav was quick to sense trouble.

He was reminded of those four black years (1992-96) when he was out of the team only because certain unsubstantiated allegations were made against him on his maiden tour of Down Under. He clearly didn't want a repeat of that and wanted to clear the air with skipper Sachin.

Sourav and Sachin met at a food court for lunch in Toronto. As usual, Sachin was on time. Not many people know that Sachin and Sourav go back a long time and they have a healthy regard for each other's ability. They know each other since their school days, having toured England together under the guidance of Kailash Ghattani, a former pace bowler of repute.

Right:
No rivalry. Both have respect for each other

Pages 62–63:
Sourav stands at ease and in front of his men before General Pervez Musharraf

Sachin appeared quite hurt by the demonstrations in Kolkata and made no bones about it during his meeting with Sourav. But when Sourav explained his position and made it clear that he was not involved with it, Sachin gracefully accepted his teammate's position. The air had been cleared and everything forgotten.

While coming back from Toronto that year, Sourav made a promise to himself—that he would do something special here when India returned to this venue next year.

He was as good as his word. On his next trip to Toronto, Sourav bagged four Man-of-the-Match Awards on the trot which is still a world record in the history of one-day cricket.

He achieved this feat in the Sahara 'Friendship Cup', which was played between India and Pakistan at Toronto from 13-21 September, 1997. So overloaded was Sourav with trophies on the return flight home that he was struggling to find space to stash his spoils in the overhead baggage cabins. Apart from the four MoM awards, Sourav had even bagged five wickets for 16 runs, which is one of the best bowling performances by an Indian against Pakistan. India, of course, won the five-match series 4-1.

At the football ground, Kolkata

It made Indian fans delirious with joy because it was not the kind of scoreline they had been used to, especially when India squared up against their traditional rivals.

Thanks to Sourav, beating Pakistan on a cricket field was no longer a big deal. Sourav's brilliant form with the bat continued and it helped India win the three-nation Silver Jubilee Independence Cup in Bangladesh in January 1998. India was contesting the best-of-three finals against Pakistan and honours were even after the first two matches. India won the first match by eight wickets only for Pakistan to draw level with a six-wicket win. The stage was set for a grand finale.

Pakistan appeared to hold the upper hand in the decider when they ran up a mammoth 314 for five in a 48-overs-per-side game. This, after Indian skipper Mohammed Azharuddin had won the toss and decided to field first.

Sourav shares a laugh during practice

No team in ODI history had chased so many runs successfully. India had no choice but to go for it. Sachin and Sourav provided a scorching start, adding 71 for the first wicket with the former scoring 41 off just 26 balls. Sourav, on the other hand, was content to stay at the wicket and played the role of a sheet-anchor to perfection. He added 179 runs for the second wicket with Robin Singh, who had been promoted in the batting order to force the pace. And when Sourav was himself out for a brilliant 124 in the 43rd over, India was on the threshold of a historic win. India needed 41 runs off 32 balls with six wickets in hand. The match wasn't quite over, but India was in the driver's seat.

However, Sourav was not satisfied with his effort. He felt that he should have seen India home and not left the task for the lower order. In the end, after a bit of drama, Hrishikesh Kanitkar and Javagal Srinath won the match for India. As soon as the winning runs were scored, Sourav was seen rushing to the ground to embrace Kanitkar and Srinath and when he was handed over the Man-of-the-Match trophy, he praised the duo's role in his acceptance speech. Pointing to his trophy he said: 'It belongs to them (Kanitkar and Srinath). They had made it possible.'

That's humility for you. No, it wasn't cheap publicity he was seeking. Sourav clearly believed that had India lost, his fabulous innings would have counted for little, nor would he have got the award. Such was the man's commitment to the team's cause. But then, Sourav has always been like that—different, and a trifle misunderstood.

Once, he had casually remarked that what was the point in making 30 hundreds if they did not win matches for India. Incidentally, Sachin, at that point in his career, had 30 one-day centuries under his belt. Sourav's critics pounced on him, saying that his caustic remark had actually been aimed at Sachin. They flayed him for trying to belittle the 'Little Master' and his achievements. Sourav was taken aback by the hostile reaction to his rather innocuous comment. For, he believed that his remark was not aimed at

Getting ready to take guard

A partnership with Sachin

anyone, let alone Sachin, by far India's most prolific run-getter and match-winner in the shorter version of the game. Sourav was hurt even more because Sachin is one cricketer whom he had always held in very high regard. He calls him, Choto babu (Little Champion). Time and again during his captaincy career, Sourav has fallen back on Sachin for advice. Once he was asked by a journalist to compare Sachin with Brian Lara. Sourav didn't even need any time to ponder over his choice. 'Sachin, of course,' he had said. 'Sachin has close to 80 international hundreds while lesser cricketers spend their entire career scoring 30. He is above everyone else. Day in and out, I have seen him from the closest possible quarter. I know his hunger for runs and the dedication and discipline that he brings to the crease,' Sourav concluded his argument. And he should know, for he was part of ODI cricket's most successful opening partnerships. With Sourav and Sachin opening the innings, Indian cricket never had it so good. So when he, as captain, broke the partnership in the larger interests of the team, he faced plenty of criticism in the media as well as from former cricketers.

Even Sunil Gavaskar was skeptical. 'India had the best possible opening partnership in one-day cricket that no opponent bowler could break. But Indians themselves have broken it,' Gavaskar had written in his newspaper column. Sourav, of course, had his reasons in doing so. Before the NatWest Trophy in England, India was experimenting with their line-up in a bid to strike the right combination and balance. Sourav was not happy with the batting order and strongly felt that Sachin would be more useful to the team if he batted at No.4. So, he persuaded Sachin to drop down in the order.

Critics, once more pounced on Sourav. They pointed at Sachin's record while batting at the top of the order and accused Sourav of being unfair to the maestro. But Sourav countered the criticism with solid cricketing logic.

'We need an experienced batsman to anchor the innings as well as take full toll of the slog overs. And who is better than Sachin to play this role? We have lost many games even after Sachin and I had given the team a good start only because there was no one down the order to make the slog overs count. We had two options—either I or Sachin dropped down the order. With Virender Sehwag starting to make his mark as an opener in Test matches, we felt he should be drafted in to open the innings in ODIs, too. With Viru as one of the openers, we preferably needed a left-handed batsman as his partner. Hence, it was decided that I would stay at the top of the order and Sachin would bat at No. 4,' Sourav explained.

Senior pro Sachin played his part to perfection. Batting at No. 4, he had two hundreds, both coming at a time the team was in trouble, vindicating Sourav's stand.

An elated Sourav had further explained his logic: 'When a batsman of Sachin's stature is at the wicket, the rival team is always under pressure. All teams want to see him back in the pavilion. Theoretically, if Sachin could bat for all 50 overs, India would rarely lose a match, but we all know that it's practically impossible for anyone to bat through all the overs each time. It is more realistic to expect that Sachin would bat through the last

The 'Little Master' watches with interest

30 overs on most occasions. That was the reason why we chose to break up our association at the top of the order. We simply wanted better results for the team.'

Sourav's decision was also prompted by the fact that both Azharuddin and Ajay Jadeja were unavailable for national duty following the match-fixing scandal. This had weakened the middle-order somewhat. However, pressures from various quarters as well as his own dipping form forced Sourav to push Sachin up the order once again. Even then the Sachin-Sourav partnership hardly ever got going.

No matter what critics say, even Sachin has always held Sourav's ability with the bat and his cricketing acumen in high esteem, so much so that when it came to choosing his successor for the top-job in Indian cricket, Sachin backed Sourav to the hilt. And playing under Sourav, Sachin always gave 100 per cent.

It's, therefore, little wonder that Sachin and Sourav between them picked up as many as 81 Man-of-the-Match Awards for India and won more games for their country than any other pair in Indian cricket. That's the stuff champions are made of.

The 'prince' becomes the 'king'

SAHARA

On his bowling run-up

Facing page:
'That's it'—
Sourav is elated

The best things in life have always come to Sourav Ganguly amid crisis and with a twist of fate. Right from his debut in first-class cricket, ODIs and Tests, providence has played a major part in Sourav's career. Nothing has ever come to him on a platter. So it was no surprise that the most coveted job in Indian cricket came his way at a time when the Indian team was scraping the bottom of the barrel, so to say.

India had lost five Test matches on the trot and seven of the eight ODIs prior to his appointment. Also, India had lost a home series after 13 years. In order to put Sourav's coronation as captain into perspective, we must go back a little in time.

The tour of Down Under by our cricketers in 1999-2000 was easily one of the low points in Indian cricket. India, under Sachin Tendulkar's captaincy came back after being badly mauled by the Aussies, both in Tests as well as the tri-series that followed. First they were outplayed 3-0 in the three-Test series and then India managed only a single victory in the tri-series.

PEPSI

There were signs of trouble even before the Indian team flew out to Australia. The selectors left out Mohammed Azharuddin, Ajay Jadeja and Nayan Mongia and packed the side with newcomers who had no experience of the Australian conditions. The Indian team management, comprising skipper Sachin and coach Kapil Dev, was at odds with the BCCI top brass, prompting the then secretary Jaywant Yashwant Lele to openly ridicule the team.

Asked by mediapersons about India's chances in Australia, Lele had retorted: 'They will lose 3-0'. The entire country reacted with disbelief at Lele's comments, which ultimately proved to be prophetic. In all, Sachin's India lost 10 out of 11 international matches they played on that tour of Down Under. The Indian players, too, were angry, but they failed to channelise their anger into quality performances on their field. Instead, they were so battered and bruised in the first two Tests that they had to call in replacements.

Rookie Andhra Pradesh wicketkeeper MSK Prasad who was preferred to the seasoned Mongia, took ill midway through the series, prompting the selectors to fly out Mongia. However, Prasad appeared to have miraculously recovered from his illness

The captains' enclosure

'We are with you, Skip'—Harbhajan Singh seems to be saying

and played on, leaving Mongia to cool his heels in the dressing room. Mongia returned without playing a single game on the tour. The message to Mongia was clear: He was not wanted in the side.

Peeved by the team management's decision to ignore Mongia, the BCCI refused to accede to their second request of sending out Jadeja in order to bolster the middle-order. The Aussies made a clean sweep of the series, leaving India to lick their wounds. It was the same old story in the tri-series and the Indian team came back totally demoralised.

The South Africans, who came to India soon after, were quick to capitalise on this and pulled off two rather easy victories in successive Test matches to become the first team to win a Test series on Indian soil after Pakistan had done so in 1987.

Pakistan's victory in the final Test in Bangalore was a narrow one despite a masterful 96 by Sunil Gavaskar on a minefield of the Chinnaswamy Stadium wicket. Hansie Cronje's men, however, didn't have to fight that hard as India caved in without displaying much spunk.

Even before the series had started, Sachin, perhaps unhappy with the way in which things had gone during his second stint as captain, had announced that he would step down at the end of the series. The selectors too were eager to make some changes in a bid to revitalise the side. So, in came Azhar, once more. But as luck would have it, Azhar picked up an injury before the first Test and had to sit it out. India lost that game in Mumbai and South Africa took a 1-0 lead in the two-Test series. Azhar returned for the next Test in Bangalore, but the script didn't change for the Indian team and they lost the match on the fifth morning. Ironically Azhar scored a century in the second innings, but it was only of academic interest.

He did not know it then, but it was to be Azhar's last Test match—his 99th. The match-fixing scandal erupted soon after the ODI series that followed and Azhar, having got embroiled in that, never got to pull on an India cap again.

God, give me strength!

Rahul Dravid listens as Sourav makes a point to Harbhajan Singh

Facing page: An autograph for a fan

Now, with Sachin declaring his intention to step down from the captaincy after the Test series, the selectors had to find a new captain. But first they had to find a vice-captain. There were two deserving candidates. One of them, Ajay Jadeja, made it clear to the selectors that he should not be considered for the vice-captain's post in case he was overlooked for the captaincy.

Sourav, therefore, became an automatic choice for the vice-captain's post. Both Sourav and Jadeja had already tasted reasonable success with the national team as stop-gap captains. Sourav had won in Toronto with a team that had no other senior player except Rahul Dravid. Yet, his team had beaten Brian Lara's West Indies in the final and when it was time to lift the trophy, Sourav invited every member of the team to the podium to share the honour as he felt it was excellent team work had helped them to win the trophy. This gesture went down extremely well with the younger players.

Jadeja, on the other hand had his share of success in Sharjah. Although India did not win the tournament there, his leadership qualities drew all-round praise. Moreover, Jadeja was 'senior' to Sourav in the sense that when Sourav was forced to return from the tour of Australia in 1991-92, Jadeja had stayed on and played in the 1992 World Cup. Moreover, he was very close to coach Kapil Dev. However, the selectors were reluctant to pass on the captaincy to Jadeja because he was still not an automatic choice in the Indian Test team and they had no brief to appoint two different captains for the two versions of the game.

It was here that Sourav got the support of outgoing captain Sachin. The Little Master had also recommended to the then chairman of the selection committee, Ajit Wadekar, that Sourav should lead the side in Toronto in 1999 when he had made himself unavailable for the ODI series. That was that, and Sourav was made the skipper four-and-a-half years after making a comeback to international cricket. The 'prince' of Kolkata had finally become the 'king' of Indian cricket.

He was lying on the floor of his room in the Taj Mahal hotel in Mumbai when the news came through. Phones started ringing relentlessly as there was a flood of congratulatory messages for the new leader. In between answering those calls, Sourav reflected on his journey in international cricket. I still remember his words, spoken almost as a soliloquy: 'Did I expect that one day I would

Facing page:
Famous Bengali actor Soumitra Chatterjee felicitates Sourav at a state goverment programme at the Netaji Indoor Stadium, Kolkata

With Bengal Chief Minister, Buddhadeb Bhattacharya and the Queen of Indian Melody, Lata Mangeshkar

get this honour when I made a comeback? How could I, when I knew very well in 1996 that I was not even a permanent member of the squad? When a player makes it to the national team, it is a dream-come-true for him. At the same time, he worries about cementing his place when he breaks into the national team. I was no exception. And I knew one failure would send me back to square one. I did not have time to think about anything else other than my next innings when I got back into the team in 1996.'

Humility personified, you might say. But it's true. My mind goes back to the summer of 1996 when I had called on him in his hotel room not long after he had cracked that historic century at Lord's. Instead of being elated, he looked relieved, but was still quite unsure about his place in the team. He had very eagerly inquired about India's next engagement and whether he stood any chance of making the team!

He was worried that even though he had played well in the Tests, he was yet to prove himself as a one-day player. And as India's next assignment was a one-day series, his fears were perhaps justified. The thought of leading the team at some stage in his career certainly would not have crossed Sourav's mind then. But in the next four years, after having scored 23 international hundreds and more than 8,500 runs in both forms of the game, Sourav was more than ready to assume the hot seat.

It was hardly an easy assignment. Having lost both the Tests to South Africa, Sourav was now required to lift a thoroughly demoralised side and take on the best one-day side in the world. After all, Cronje's South African team boasted a success rate of more than 75 per cent in ODIs. A tall order for any captain. But, Sourav began with a bang.

The skipper himself was a bit tense in the opening match at Kochi, but marshalled his resources brilliantly. He even got

Waiting for the next batsman

Dravid to bowl off-break to confuse the Proteas. Azharuddin and Jadeja then batted superbly and India won the match narrowly. A winning start was all that mattered and skipper Sourav came into his own at the Keenan Stadium in Jamshedpur.

Till then, India had never won an ODI in the Steel City. Sourav decided to change all that and scored a brilliant century during the course of which he put the South African bowling to sword. It was enough to put India 2-0 ahead in the series. And although India had lost the next match, they clinched the series in the fourth game. South Africa won the inconsequential final game to leave India victors by a 3-2 margin.

Unfortunately, Sourav's first series as a full-fledged captain will be remembered for all the wrong reasons as subsequently it was revealed that at least certain attempts were made by a few South African players, including their captain Cronje, to fix matches.

When the match-fixing charges against Cronje surfaced, Sourav could not believe it.

'I could not believe it. Almost all the matches saw brilliant batting displays and more than 500 runs were scored in all the matches by both sides. It was a highly competitive series. At least I was happy that nobody from our camp was questioned. I tried to ensure a good environment in the dressing room so that the players could give their best.'

Indian cricket went through a torrid time during which they lost quite a few senior players including Azhar. It called for a strong leader to show the way and Sourav was not found wanting. His leadership qualities were further highlighted when India went to Nairobi to take part in the Champions Trophy, also known as the 'Mini World Cup'. Being a knock-out tournament where a team would have to return home after losing, it was crunch time for Sourav and his boys.

Their first match was against the Kenyans, who were duly sent packing. Next up were the mighty Australians under Steve Waugh. The Aussies were the world champions and they were eager to assert their supremacy in one-day cricket. Moreover, they wanted revenge as well as the trophy which had eluded them in Bangladesh in 1998 when they were beaten by India in their very first game.

The Indians were, however, up for the challenge. Young Yuvraj Singh had caught the eye of the skipper, who was instrumental in getting him on board for the African safari. This youthful lad had not come with any baggage. Sourav, decided to throw him into action against the formidable Aussies. Yuvi, as he is lovingly known to his mates, proved his skipper right by playing brilliantly under extreme pressure. He pulled and hooked Australian speedsters, including Glenn McGrath, with disdain to raise hopes of an Indian victory. Next, it was the turn of another rookie to show his class against the Aussies. Baroda's left-arm pacer Zaheer Khan not only opened the bowling but also worked up a fair bit of pace. Here was one bowler who regularly hit the deck and pitched his yorkers bang on target. Even the experienced Steve Waugh had no answers and India marched into the semi-final.

The South Africans were next in line. This time, it was the skipper who batted right through the innings to score another wonderful hundred that virtually paved the way for his team's entry into the final. The Proteas made a bold attempt to overhaul the Indian total, but with Herschelle Gibbs retiring hurt when going great guns, Sourav's boys managed to clinch the issue. Now they only had to beat New Zealand to bring the trophy home.

Sourav continued his great form in the final, too, scoring another hundred. However, Sourav was involved in two crucial run outs during that innings that sent Dravid and Sachin back to the pavilion. His running between the wickets came in for much criticism, but his century had helped India set up what was considered to be a winning total. Chris Cairns, however, had other ideas. Having sustained an injury which had him batting on virtually one leg, Cairns often took the aerial route and dealt mostly in fours and sixes. He hit everything with the middle of his bat and slowly took the game away from India's grasp. It was certainly one of the best knocks played in New Zealand's cricket history and it broke Indian hearts.

To this day, Sourav remembers Cairns' magnificent innings. 'I just could not believe it. He was just unstoppable. I tried every bowler, every combination, but nothing could stop him from winning the match for his team. It's one of the greatest ODI knocks I have seen,' he recollected.

Cairns' innings had the same demoralising effect on the Indians as the last-ball six by Javed Miandad in Sharjah off Chetan Sharma. It sure took Sourav and his team some time to recover from the shock!

Captain Courageous KOs the Aussies

In 2001, Steve Waugh came to India with a definite aim of conquering what he had described as the 'Last Frontier'. Having won against every side both at home and abroad, the Aussies came to India hoping to stretch their winning streak from 15 to 18. And skipper Waugh made it known in no uncertain terms after setting his foot on Indian soil.

Winning in India is the ultimate challenge for any team. Australia's otherwise impressive international record lacked a series win in India. After all, the Australians had not won a Test series in India

With Steve Waugh before the toss—a contentious issue between them—during the tour of Australia in 2003-04

'Well done mate!' Sourav to Anil Kumble

after 1969. Probably that's why Waugh had termed it the 'Last Frontier'. And he wanted to conquer it. He had, therefore, come with the best available side that was well prepared to achieve the desired results. The Aussies had also brought along ice-vests to counter the heat and humidity in India, their own chefs and drinking water, which showed how determined they were to conquer the conditions here before conquering on the pitch. Having won their last 15 Tests, they were a confident lot, too.

Given their form over the past year or so, the entire cricket fraternity was convinced that no team could contain the Aussies, let alone defeat them. Steve Waugh's men were being talked about in the same breath as the invincible West Indians of the late 1970s and early '80s. And despite India's great record at home, they were clearly the underdogs going into the three-Test series. You could hardly blame the pundits for backing Australia, for Waugh's was

Making a point—over there

a well-balanced side, rich in experience. With Matthew Hayden, Michael Slater, Justin Langer, Mark Waugh, Ricky Ponting and Steve Waugh as the specialist batsmen, Adam Gilchrist, as the murderous wicketkeeper-batsman, Glenn McGrath, Jason Gillespie, Michael Kasprowicz as the fast bowlers and the 'king of spin' Shane Warne in the side, any captain would fancy his chances even against a World XI. And the Indian squad hardly resembled one.

They had a relatively new captain in Sourav Ganguly, who was just one Test match old, having led India to an improbable victory in Bangladesh's debut Test in Dhaka. They had a new coach in New Zealander John Wright, the first foreigner to be appointed by the BCCI in that position. They had a new opening pair in Sadgopan Ramesh and Shiv Sundar Das. But more importantly, they didn't have the services of Anil Kumble, the country's most successful spinner and a proven match-winner on home soil.

Kumble was struggling with injuries and his place was finally assigned to a talented upcoming off-spinner Harbhajan Singh, even though the selectors had initially favoured Delhi's Sharandeep Singh. Sharandeep was even given a chance to bowl against the Aussies during a warm-up game, but it took skipper Sourav's phenomenal persuasive powers to get Harbhajan, nicknamed Bhajji by his teammates, into the first XI.

It was hardly the best Indian team to take on the mighty Aussies. In fact, in 1998 when Mark Taylor had come to India with a similar vision to Waugh's, the Indian team had a much fuller look to it. Kumble was fully fit. Navjot Singh Sidhu had been in great form as an opener. Skipper Mohammed Azharuddin's presence in the

Three's company: John Wright, Rahul Dravid and Sourav

Anil Kumble does it again. Sourav is elated

middle-order had lent solidity to the batting line up. Moreover, Azhar being the blue-eyed boy of the BCCI, always got the kind of wickets that suited his team most.

Poor Sourav never had that luxury, for in his era, the International Cricket Council had become more stringent and the emphasis was on preparing sporting wickets. So, the odds had really stacked up against Sourav and his team before the start of the series.

Sourav, however, had done his homework on the Aussies. He decided to give back to the Aussies as they gave. So, no sooner had Waugh spoken about extending their winning run from 15 to 18, Sourav, in an interview to the Indian media, rubbished Waugh's claims and said the Australian captain can forget the numbers 16, 17 and 18! Such a counter-attack from an Indian

You need more than one head to lead India. Will four do?

captain was unseen or unheard of and the Aussies had taken an early hit in the exchange of verbal volleys.

A great supporter of the Brazilian football team, Sourav, much like the samba boys, decided to go on all-out attack against arguably the best side in the world. He attacked the Aussies verbally both on and off the field. The Aussies, so used to sledging against other teams, found themselves at the receiving end. And mind you, it wasn't ugly sledging by the Indian players. There was an element of wit involved in their comments which had the Aussies hopping mad.

For example, Indian close-in fielders often taunted Slater and Langer saying, 'How about scoring some runs outside Australia, mate?' And some of them even had the cheek to 'warn' Warne that even 'Hampshire would not take you after this series'! Amusing stuff really, but Waugh was hardly smiling when he was apparently left waiting for five to ten minutes by Sourav before emerging from the dressing room for the toss before the Test matches.

Celebrating the win over Australia, in Chennai

Waugh obviously did not like to be stood up by the host captain and went and spilled the beans to the media, thereby giving birth to a full blown controversy. The Australian media, quite expectedly, went to town with these incidents and criticised the Indian captain. Waugh also got plenty of support from the Indian media. Most newspapers and TV channels took Sourav to task for his 'ungentlemanly' behaviour without even bothering to check their facts with the skipper.

When I asked Sourav about those incidents, he explained the entire episode. 'Actually, it was a trick played by Steve. He intentionally used to arrive five-ten minutes earlier than the scheduled time for the toss in a bid to show to the world media how unprepared I was. As I had no control over his actions, I simply decided to stick to my schedule, but made sure that I was not late for the toss,' Sourav said. 'I am aware of cricket's best traditions. I was brought up in a cricketing environment. Believe me, I could do nothing to avoid this unsavoury controversy. Before I knew what was happening, it had become an international issue,' he added. The Test series, therefore got off to a rather spicy start, but India buckled quite easily under the Aussie onslaught and Waugh had a big grin on his usually poker face after winning the first Test in Mumbai within three days. The wicket at the Wankhede Stadium suited the Aussies more than the Indians and Adam Gilchrist perhaps played his best knock on foreign soil. It was his hundred that helped the Aussies to post 349 in the first innings. Then their bowlers took over. India batted poorly in both innings and Australia coasted to a 10-wicket victory to go up 1-0 in the series. It certainly looked at that stage that the Last Frontier would be conquered by Waugh's men. And nothing happened on the first three days of the Kolkata Test to suggest that the script would change for the Indian team.

Steve Waugh played a typically gritty knock to rescue his team despite Harbhajan Singh's maiden hat-trick in Test cricket. Of all people, Jason Gillespie gave Waugh good support and the Aussies posted 445 in their first innings. The Indians, perhaps still overawed by the opposition, caved in meekly for 171 and were forced to follow on. The only notable contribution in the first innings came off Vangipurappu Venkata Sai Laxman's bat. He remained not out on 59. This, coupled with his past record against the Aussies (a fabulous 167 in the Sydney Test in 1999) perhaps prompted skipper Sourav and coach Wright to send him in at No. 3 in the second innings.

Sourav later explained their rationale: 'We felt as he was in good nick, he should be allowed to bat higher up the order. We also knew that if Laxman stays at the crease for some time, runs were bound to come quickly. That would reduce the pressure on the batsmen to follow. Moreover, Dravid also being capable of holding up one end, it made sense to reshuffle the batting order,' said Sourav. However, at the end of the third day's play, another defeat for India loomed large.

The openers had gone cheaply; Sourav tried his best to hang around, but fell to Waugh; Sachin managed just 10, leaving the last recognised pair of batsmen Laxman and Dravid at the

crease. The Aussies had already started celebrating at the end of the third day in anticipation of their series win.

Sourav with former India coach John Wright

What happened on the fourth day was not only unthinkable, but also unbelievable. For, nothing remotely like this had happened in Indian cricket history. Laxman and Dravid played the innings of their lives and remained unbeaten throughout the day. They went on to add 276 runs for the fifth wicket to bring India back into the game. So impressive was Laxman in that innings of 281 that Ian Chappell described it as 'Very Very Special'. During the course of his historic innings, Laxman surpassed Sunil Gavaskar's 236 not out scored in Chennai against the West Indies in 1983-84 and 281 became the new benchmark for Indian batsmen.

It's sad that Dravid's supporting role got relegated to the background in the face of Laxman's superlative effort. However, Dravid's 180 was worth its weight in gold and it helped India, not only to make up the first innings deficit, but also set Australia some sort of a target to chase. Sourav declared India's second innings closed on 657 for seven, setting Australia a winning target of 384 runs. It was an unbelievable turn of events that turned the Test on its head.

The Aussies had gone from being the hunters to the hunted in course of just a day's play. Harbhajan completed what was a fairy tale victory for India on the final day. Bhajji was simply unplayable. The Aussies were not used to such conditions where they had to defend to save the test on the fifth day and they cut a sorry figure. Players like Gilchrist, brought up on heady success, simply could not withstand the pressure applied by the Indian bowlers and fielders and were unable to survive in front of the packed Eden Gardens galleries. Australia lost by 171 after enforcing the follow-on and the series was level at 1-1 before the final Test in Chennai. More importantly, Australia's winning streak was halted after 16.

As usual, Chennai saw Tendulkar at his best once again. He scored a risk-free hundred there and Harbhajan's golden arm picked up wickets almost at will. Hayden's heroics could not save the Aussies. After his century in the first Test, Gilchrist just could never reach double figures and Ponting could not get away from Bhajji's clutches as the Australian batting struggled to come to terms with the Indian spin attack. Rejuvenated by that miracle win in Kolkata, the Indian team started believing that that they could topple the Aussies.

The visitors set India a small target to chase in the last innings and fought hard to win the series, but another Laxman special (a half-century) at a critical time saved India the blushes. The last few winning runs were chalked up by Bhajji, India's premier bowler who had taken 32 wickets in the three-Test series, and wicketkeeper Sameer Dighe.

Waugh had to return empty-handed and with a broken heart as the 'Last Frontier' remained unconquered. Aussies have always been bad losers and it was no surprise that Waugh had nothing good to say about India's tremendous fight back, instead he heaped scorn on his rival skipper when the Australian media wanted his reactions on the loss of the series.

If Waugh's reaction was on expected lines, the Indian media's attitude towards their winning captain was baffling to say the least. Clearly, not used to an Indian skipper paying back his rival in the same coin, they found faults with Sourav's aggression on the field. Perhaps, they would have been happier had the Indian skipper given in tamely to the Aussies and been gallant in defeat instead of leading from the front.

True, Sourav did not have a great series with the bat. The Aussie bowlers provoked him on the off-side, arguably his strongest area, and managed to get the better of him, but as a leader of men, he gave the team direction and inculcated among his teammates a zeal to win.

Facing page:
Addressing the media

A new leader had arrived in world cricket and under him a new Team India begun to take shape. Sourav's leadership qualities had impressed the late Freddie Trueman so much that he had advised the then English skipper Nasser Hussain to 'do a Sourav Ganguly' in the upcoming Ashes series against Australia.

All this, however, failed to convince the Indian selectors about Sourav's worth as a skipper. Instead of appointing him as the captain for a long term, they continued to extend his rein from series to series. That is Indian cricket for you. Sourav was hardly heartbroken, though. He realised the enormity of his team's achievement and savoured the triumph before plotting the downfall of India's next rival.

Indian cricket's Captain Courageous had arrived and the world could see this.

Sourav is overjoyed
—a catch is taken

STAR
ESPN
NDTV

On a high Down Under

Apart from the home series against Australia in 2001, under Sourav Ganguly, India played two other Test series against Australia: one Down Under in 2003-04 and the other in 2004-05 in India. While India drew the series in Australia, they surrendered the 'Last Frontier' at home after 35 long years.

Traditionally, India has always been hard to beat in home conditions, but extremely vulnerable away from home. A quick look at India's record in Australia will show that barring in 1980-81 when India under Sunil Gavaskar had managed to draw the three-Test series 1-1, they have always come out second best. Yes, India did win two Test matches Down Under with Bishen Singh Bedi in charge, but they ultimately lost the series 2-3 against an Australian side led by Bobby Simpson, who had been lured out of retirement to take charge of a rag-tag outfit as all their top cricketers were busy playing in World Series Cricket introduced by TV magnate Kerry Packer.

Dean Jones gets Adam Gilchrist and Sourav to share their thoughts after the toss

The Indian huddle

Even without their top 30 players, Australia still managed to win the series. Such was the state of Indian cricket in 1977-78. Sourav was determined to taste success in a Test series in Australia. He targeted the India tour of Down Under in 2003-04 to achieve this and started planning things quite early. Few months before the tour, Sourav made a quiet trip to Sydney to meet Greg Chappell. He wanted Chappell to iron out minor flaws in his batting as well as prepare him to succeed on Australian wickets. He spent a week with Chappell and came back suitably impressed with the Australian's method of coaching and philosophy about batting. And by the time, he landed in Australia with his team, Sourav had it all worked out in his mind. The formula for success only needed to be applied in match situations.

The first Test was at Gabba, Brisbane. Australia's game plan was to play on the faster, bouncier tracks first and take a 2-0 lead. The pressure would then tell on the visiting side and they would cave under it. After what had happened in India, the Aussies were clearly not ready to take any chances.

Things went their way early on in the Brisbane Test with Indian batsmen struggling to cope with the bounce. On top of it, Sachin

Tendulkar got a rank bad decision from West Indies umpire Steve Bucknor who ruled him out lbw when the ball was clearly missing the stumps.

It was the time for the Indian captain to stand up and deliver. He did. Sourav proved his worth and answered his critics by scoring a gallant 144. Even his staunchest critics rate this as his best Test innings after his consecutive hundreds on Test debut. None of the Australian bowlers could disrupt his rhythm. He played a lot straighter and hit the ball in the 'V'. This pleased Chappell most. Sourav had clearly benefited from his personal coaching when he had come down to Sydney.

In cricket, pundits say that while playing away from home, always make sure that you make a confident start to the series. If you lose the first one, the team's morale is shattered and everything tends to spin out of control. That's what had happened to the Indian team touring Australia in 1999-00. The Tendulkar-led side had lost the first Test in no time and thereafter failed to lift their

After a good day on the ground, with VVS Laxman

Anil Kumble's spin punch fells yet another

game sufficiently to stage a comeback in the series which they ultimately lost 3-0. However, this time it was different.

A splendid century from their skipper had ensured an honourable draw and a confident start to the series. In the next Test at Adelaide, it was Rahul Dravid's turn to get a big score. Dravid hit a double-century while VVS Laxman added another hundred to his kitty against the Aussies to give India a solid base. He also anchored the second innings well to help India win the second Test and go 1-0 up in the series.

Skipper Sourav was at his inspirational best. This time he chose to make a man out of a boy. He simply threw the new ball to teenage left-arm fast bowler Irfan Pathan and asked him to do the job for his country. Pathan dealt key blows and Australia caved in. Sourav later recalled what Pakistan great Wasim Akram had once advised him: 'Throw them (youngsters) at the deep end of the pool if you feel that they are dying to perform. Do not hold them back if you think they are capable of taking on the best.'

The Indian skipper did just that and Pathan showed plenty of guts and gumption as a result of which the unthinkable had happened—for the first time in a decade, the Australians were behind 0-1 after two Tests on home soil. Putting pressure on their opponents is a ploy generally employed by the Aussies when they are on tour. Sourav merely took a leaf out of Australia's book and returned the compliment.

In all humility Sourav said that he still maintained that the Australians were undoubtedly the best team in the world, but as India had beaten them thrice in the last five Test matches, his young team was now a true challenger to Australia's No. 1 standing in Test cricket.

Sourav's comments caused a furore in the world of cricket. The Australian media was harsh on their skipper who found himself at the receiving end, both on and off the field. The Australian media perhaps twisted Sourav's comments a bit to suit their agenda and needled the home side. They misquoted Sourav as having said: 'We are the world's best team now.'

Ricky Ponting, who had regained his touch in the series in the absence of his nemesis, the injured Harbhajan Singh, was the first to break his silence on this issue. Ponting taunted the Indian skipper and his team by suggesting that India should win a few away series before laying their claim to the 'best team' title. What the future Aussie captain had perhaps overlooked was the fact

With Greg Chappell at the nets. Notice the protective band on his right elbow

that the Indians were really playing well abroad as well. India had won a Test in Kandy, Port-of-Spain and Headingley. They had also drawn a Test series in England before arriving in Australia. And mind you, Sourav had not claimed the No. 1 ranking for his team, but only due recognition for having beaten Australia thrice in five Tests.

Ponting's retort was typical of an Australian player. For the first time in many years, the near-invincible Aussies were being really threatened by a new power in international cricket. Hell broke loose at the end of the first day's play in the third Test match. The Indians were comfortably placed with 300-plus on the board and plenty of batting to follow. Virender Sehwag was at his devastating best in Melbourne. The MCG is one of the biggest grounds in the world and it was here that Viru had scored 195 in a day. He would have got more had he not holed out in the deep while trying to bring up his double-century with a six.

Viru's onslaught had left the Aussies shaken. The Delhi opener had literally toyed with the Australian attack which was missing both Glenn McGrath and Shane Warne. This particular series also exploded the myth about Australia's great supply-line of players from a great system that makes tall claims about spotting and nurturing talents.

The Indians, however, failed to capitalise on that start. Sachin failed again, so did Sourav the next morning. Had Sourav, the last of the recognised batsmen in the side, batted for two hours more that morning, his team would have come back from Australia having created history. But that was not to be. Ponting batted well once again. The Indian bowling attack sans Bhajji and Zaheer Khan looked rather ordinary and the Aussies took full toll. Sourav batted beautifully in the second innings. He was also hailed in the media for his bold decision to promote himself up the order. In that innings he came to bat even before Tendulkar, who had till then looked totally out of sorts. By choosing to take on the Australian pace attack head on, the Indian captain had also managed to keep Tendulkar handy for a late assault on the Aussie bowlers the next morning. But Sachin failed again and Sourav tried in vain to save the Boxing Day Test.

Before the last Test in Sydney, which was to be the last one for Steve Waugh, the series was tied 1-1 and there were hopes in the Indian dressing room that they might be able to pull off a series win here as the Sydney Cricket Ground (SCG) wicket traditionally helps the spinners.

The New Year (2004) brought loads of runs for the Little Maestro. Sachin played cautiously to make a splendid double-century (242), by far his best Test innings Down Under. And with Laxman scoring another brilliant hundred, Indians piled up more than

700 runs on the board! The Aussies tried their best but could not avoid the follow-on. Skipper Sourav, however, decided against enforcing it as his main strike bowler Anil Kumble was dead tired and the rookies also needed some rest. Sourav, therefore, decided to play it safe as he did not want to lose the series. So, India batted a second time to ensure that they would not lose the series.

Steve played the last of his Waugh-like innings to save the Test for his team while Simon Katich lent him very good support at the other end. When Waugh finally fell to Kumble, the Australians were safe. Waugh got a standing ovation from the crowd for his long and distinguished service to Australian cricket. The Indian players, too returned with their heads held high and richly deserved the accolades that poured in from all corners.

The Australians, of course, bounced right back from this setback. When they returned to India to play a four-Test series in September 2004, they had a new captain and new ideas to make their mission

Facing page:
At a picturesque ground in South Africa before the start of the match

Making a point to Wasim Akram; Harbhajan Singh and Dav Whatmore are also listening

successful. As it turned out, the Aussies managed to conquer the 'Last Frontier' on their third serious attempt and Team India and the BCCI, in the midst of a power struggle, played perfect hosts, offering them the kind of wickets they preferred. So surprised were the Aussies on seeing a green-top in Nagpur, which hosted the third Test that their acting-captain Adam Gilchrist, went on record saying, 'it was more like Perth!'

Sourav had a rough time during the series. He had picked up an injury even before the series got under way, but got himself fit and played in the first two Tests. India had lost the first, while rain had prevented them from winning the second. India came to Nagpur with the dream of drawing level, but the green-top made the players see red. They could not believe that they were playing in India and not England or New Zealand. It was the kind of wicket that suited the Aussies to the 'T' and they made full use of it to register a comprehensive win here. The win also gave the Aussies the series and with it their dream of conquering the 'Last Frontier' was realised.

Sourav, of course, did not play the last two Tests because of an injury. But a large section of Indian media believed that he had opted out of the Nagpur Test after failing to get the grass on the wicket shaved off before the match. His critics, as usual, claimed that Sourav was suffering from 'grassititis'. They conveniently overlooked the fact that he has Test hundreds at the Gabba, Headingley and Durban.

The final Test in Mumbai was rendered inconsequential. The wicket at the Wankhede Stadium was in a pathetic state. Forty wickets tumbled in three days, prompting the Aussies to stamp on the pitch on the fourth evening. However, no one highlighted the fact that the world champions had failed to make 100-odd runs in the fourth innings of a Test match.

The win in Mumbai came as a sort of face-saver for India. There was nobody to explain why the Nagpur pitch was made to suit the Aussies. Would India get a spin-friendly pitch in Perth? Never. But that was the kind of fait accompli that the Indian team was given in Nagpur.

In this personal ego clash, the national team's interest was sacrificed and the Aussies went home whistling a victory tune.

Sourav had captained in nine Test matches against the world champions—winning three, losing three and drawing three. This was the high point for Sourav.

BCCI
206

The making of Team India

Volleyball in Bangladesh, playing the setter

India were a reasonably good side even before Sourav Ganguly took over the captaincy. Sourav should get most of the credit for turning this unit into a winning combination by effecting some key changes.

One-day cricket is necessarily a batsman's game. And India has always been hampered by the lack of a quality all-rounder after Kapil Dev retired from the game. Every Indian captain since, has moaned the lack of a genuine jack-of-all-trades and blamed the loss of close matches on this non-existent quotient.

It was easy for captains when Kapil was around, but after that golden era successive Indian captains had failed to reorganise their forces, discounting the versatility that a quality all-rounder brings to any side. An inventive captain simply cannot sit back and lament about lack of resources, but tries his best to find an alternative path.

Initially, skipper Sourav had laid much emphasis on unearthing an all-rounder. He initially backed Ajit Agarkar and Yuvraj Singh to develop their all-round skills. But both, despite being enormously gifted, did not quite measure up to the task. While Yuvraj's left-arm spin was found to be too batsmen-friendly, especially to those who could use their feet to the spinners, Agarkar's bowling lost much of the sting after his first 50 one-day internationals. Both also lacked consistency and their form at times fluctuated such a lot that they were soon fighting to keep their places in the team.

Another problem that Sourav needed to address was in the wicketkeeping department. The Indian team needed a keeper who could contribute with the bat as well. Numerous wicketkeepers were tried out. Sameer Dighe, Saba Karim, Deep Dasgupta and Ajay Ratra all had their chances, but nobody could settle down into that role. So, Sourav had to find another option.

Perhaps that was the reason why Sourav decided to persuade Rahul Dravid to keep wickets. Sourav's logic was simple. If a top-order batsman like Dravid could double up as a wicket-keeper, he could play an extra batsman in the final XI. Dravid, who used to keep wickets in his school days, never did so in first-class cricket. So, it was hard to convince him to take up the job in international cricket.

Another reason which may have prompted Sourav to ask Dravid to keep the wickets was that the Karnataka stalwart was struggling a bit in one-day cricket. He was taking too much time to settle down, as a result of which, the innings was losing momentum. The selectors were not happy about this and wanted

Pages 116–117: We are one; we are Team India

Well bowled Sourav!

24
20
10

to drop Dravid from the ODI squad. Sourav, however, would have none of it. He told the selectors in no uncertain terms that Dravid was too good a batsman to be dropped. Sourav, however, knew that unless another option was created, the selectors would ultimately have their way. And the only way to make Dravid's position safe was to convince him to keep wickets. Also, if Dravid took up the additional responsibility Sourav could fit Mohammed Kaif, the best fielder in the country, into the side at No. 7.

Sourav has always believed in playing to his strengths. He believed that as India's strength was batting, they should play seven batsmen, with one of them keeping wickets, and four specialist bowlers. Sachin, Sehwag and the skipper himself would chip in to complete the fifth bowler's quota of 10 overs.

Dravid was very reluctant to don the big gloves initially, but ultimately gave in and did a wonderful job for the team. Dravid's reluctance was understandable. Even Sehwag had been equally apprehensive when Sourav had requested the Delhi batsman to open the innings in Test matches. Sehwag agreed to take up the offer only after Sourav had assured him that if he failed as an opener in three successive Tests, he would definitely get back his position in the middle order.

Sehwag, therefore approached his new role in a positive frame of mind and the rest, as they say, is history. Sehwag has

not looked back ever since and his record as an opener is only second to the legendary Sunil Gavaskar. That one bold move by Sourav not only opened up a new avenue for Sehwag who scored runs almost at will, but also helped India to force the issue against their opponents as the new opener being a free-stroking batsman, got his runs quite quickly.

Back to the pavilion after a hard day's work

Facing page: Moments of joy

As usual, Sourav had taken plenty of flak from the purists for trying to convert Sehwag into an opener. Opening the innings in Test matches being a specialist task, they argued that Sehwag, with his suspect technique, would not fit the bill. But thereafter, even Sourav's detractors could not think of an Indian squad without Sehwag as an opener. Things can change dramatically in Indian cricket, but it needs someone to take a few bold decisions. Sehwag's success was actually Sourav's success as had the Nawab of Najafgarh had not been approached to open the innings in Tests, he would have had to wait in the wings for a vacancy in an already crowded middle-order.

And who knows, the wait could have left Sehwag so frustrated that he could have simply faded away from the mainstream or even retired without having played many Tests. The world of cricket would have surely been poorer for it. But Sehwag was destined for greatness and his skipper had only provided him with the right platform to showcase his considerable talent.

As in Sehwag's case, Sourav could foresee Dravid's success in his dual role in the NatWest Trophy one-day tournament where Indians were up against Sri Lanka and hosts England. It turned out to be a landmark series in Indian cricket for more reasons than one. It was in this tournament that Sachin was asked to go down in the batting order to provide solidity to the middle-order. Dravid, albeit reluctantly, had agreed to stand behind the stumps, allowing Kaif to come into the playing XI at No. 7.

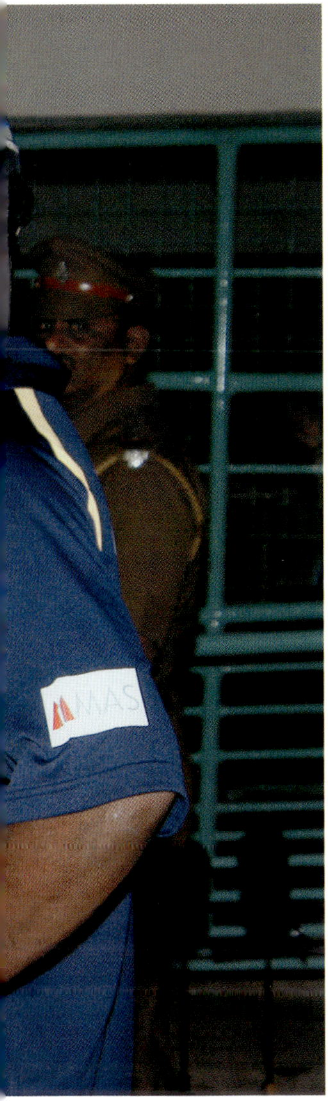

India looked a solid outfit, winning five matches in the tournament while losing only once to England when Ronnie Irani bowled a dream spell. Not only that, Sachin showed he could finish matches or could help India reach a safer total while batting first. He scored two hundreds batting at that No. 4 where many had felt he would be unable to get big scores. These critics were more worried about the number of centuries Sachin could score while Sourav wanted his best batsman to do the job for the team where a match-winning 70 would be more precious than a hundred in a losing cause.

With Kaif in the side, India's fielding acquired sharpness and batting more depth. This was proved in the final where India had to chase a world record target. Nasser Hussain, the England captain, had won the toss and elected to bat on a benign Lord's wicket. Hussain who was in great form in the Test series as well, found an able partner in Marcus Trescothick. Both batsmen scored hundreds and England piled 325 for five in their 50 overs, thoroughly demoralising the Indian fans who feared another defeat in the final.

With Mutthiah Muralidharan

Above right: Captains' corner... before an ICC meeting at Lord's.

Sourav had not been batting well in the series. But on that day, he decided to go after the English bowling and made a quick-fire 60 to provide India a flying start. Sehwag and Sourav added 106 for the opening wicket in 14.3 overs to raise visions of a great victory. However, the pressure appeared to get to the team and they suffered a mini collapse in the middle-order. Dinesh Mongia, Sachin Tendulkar and Rahul Dravid all failed, reducing India to 146 for five in 24 overs.

Yuvraj Singh then settled down and displayed a wide array of strokes and Kaif was happy to play a supporting role. This revived spirits in the Indian dressing room. But just when it seemed that Yuvraj and Kaif would take India home, the former got out. So upset was Yuvi at his dismissal that he had to almost drag himself back to the pavilion. Harbhajan came in next. Kaif, being the senior partner now, took upon himself the task of seeing India through. It was still anybody's game with 59 needed off 50 balls with four wickets standing. Bhajji did his best to provide the required support and the duo added 47 runs for the seventh wicket. Andrew Flintoff struck two telling blows in the 48th over, removing Harbhajan and Anil Kumble in the same over to reduce India to 314 for eight. However, Kaif finished the job in the company of Zaheer Khan. India had won a final after a long time and created history as well.

Skipper Sourav was delirious with joy. In a rare show of raw emotion, he took off his shirt and started waving it on the Lord's

Putting a finger to a problem

balcony. It was Sourav's way of returning the compliment to Flintoff, who had done much the same at the Wankhede Stadium in Mumbai in 2001-02. After making his point, Sourav rushed to the ground and jumped straight into the lap of Kaif.

Once more, the Indian media took Sourav to task for his apparently unsportsmanlike behaviour. Ironically, these very people had found nothing wrong with Flintoff's bare-chested act in Mumbai. They were worried about an Indian captain breaking a tradition at Lord's. Such was the double-standards of armchair critics.

Two years later, the curator of the Lord's museum approached Sourav for that shirt. Sourav duly obliged and that piece of clothing is still on display at the museum.

Kaif, who returned home as a hero, had to perform another rescue act in the ICC Champions Trophy in Sri Lanka a few months later. In the very first match of the tournament, India was on the verge of being knocked out by Zimbabwe. This time, Kaif played even better and notched up his maiden one-day hundred in the process. Sourav's seven batsmen formula had succeeded once more, but instead of getting his due recognition for initiating path-breaking moves, Sourav always got the rough end of the stick. Each time he would come back after winning a series, he would have to wait for the selectors to appoint him captain for the next series.

India didn't quite win the Champions Trophy, but were declared joint winners with Sri Lanka after rain ruined the final that was played and replayed over two days but no result could be achieved.

On the first day of the final, Indians really bowled well to restrict Sri Lanka to 230-odd, but when it was their chance to chase, it began to rain so heavily that the match had to be replayed the next day. It was the same story again. Sri Lanka won the toss and batted first. This time, they were restricted to an even smaller total, but before India could launch their chase, it started pouring heavily. Sourav, realised that he was not destined to lift the trophy. In 2000, he was denied by Chris Cairns in the final and now nature had conspired to deny his team a shot at glory. He was, therefore, content to share the trophy with the Sri Lankan captain Sanath Jayasuriya. A new Team India had begun to emerge under Sourav.

Indians then went on a highly forgettable tour of New Zealand. The Indian captain ran into early trouble on the tour when he and Harbhajan Singh were detained at the airport for carrying unclean practice shoes in their kits. There was a general alert worldwide about the foot and mouth disease and the New Zealand government was strict in enforcing

Let the next man come in

quarantine measures. Both Sourav and Harbhajan should have known better, but as is the case with government officials, the immigration officers at the airport made a big fuss out of it and the media lapped it all up. They had a rather juicy story even before the Indian team had landed in Kiwiland.

Soon after the tour started, the New Zealand Cricket Board declared that it had run out of money and stopped paying the

Indian cricketers their daily allowances. On top of it, the team hotel refused to do the team's laundry. The Indian team manager had to carry all the dirty clothes to a nearby laundry shop to get them cleaned after practice sessions and matches. The NZ Cricket Board's ineptitude was glaring.

On the cricketing front, the pitches provided in the series were all green-tops, full of pace and bounce. In the two-Test series only four batsmen could go past fifty and just one of them could reach three figures. Winning the toss was the most important thing on that tour but Sourav, who has always had bad luck with the spin of the coin, failed on that count in both the Tests.

Stephen Fleming, who must consider himself a trifle lucky to have been retained as captain for the series by the NZ Cricket Board despite his poor form, managed to sweep the Test series 2-0.

In the ODI series that followed, the pitches were no different. So green were the pitches that one could hardly differentiate it from the outfield. It was therefore no surprise that the Kiwis thrashed India. Only Sehwag scored two hundreds in the one-dayers. But for those two innings, India could take no positives out from the tour as they left for South Africa where the 2003 World Cup was to be played.

The results in New Zealand were so poor that India could only have fared better in the World Cup. At least, their skipper was confident that it would be a different India in the World Cup. And he wasn't talking through his hat.

B*ees saal baad*, a heartbreak

All the President's men

The cricket World Cup may not be as grand as the World Cup of soccer, but for Indians it's very, very special. For, it's the biggest competition in international sport where India has always fancied their chances of winning the trophy. Hopes of millions of Indians fan were rekindled in 1983 by Kapil's Devils, who 'conquered' the world and brought the Cup home.

Every Indian cricketer aspires to represent his country in the World Cup. That's what makes the ICC's quadrennial showpiece the mother of all competitions as far as Indians are concerned.

Sourav Ganguly made his World Cup debut in 1999 in England. By then, he had already established himself as an opener in ODIs who could also bowl a bit. Mohammed Azharuddin, his captain in 1996 when he had scored a century on Test debut at Lord's, was in charge again in the 1999 World Cup. And Azhar knew Sourav would be quite a handful in English conditions with his gentle medium-pace.

In fact, his bowling ability in Toronto a few years ago had prompted Sunil Gavaskar to dub him as 'the man with a golden arm'. Ever since, every time a captain needed to break a crucial partnership he would invariably turn to Sourav. And the man with a golden arm would, more often than not, oblige. Sourav was pretty upbeat about his own as well as his team's chances in England. His confidence stemmed from his super success in English conditions since 1992. Every season he would

A jubiliant Indian Team

go to England to play club cricket till he came into his own in the Summer of '96. And he always possessed a big-match temperament. Sourav, being an instinctive player, simply believes in rising to the occasion. For him, it's always mind over matter.

So, it was not at all surprising to see Sourav starting his World Cup campaign with a courageous 97 against South Africa at Hove. It was early summer in England. The weather helped the seam bowlers considerably. And after Sachin's cheap dismissal, Sourav just anchored the Indian innings. However, at the death, when there was a need to go for the big shots, a terrible misunderstanding between Sourav and Azhar left the former stranded. Sourav, thus failed to become the first Indian batsman to score a hundred on World Cup debut. India, however, lost the match to get off to a bad start. But worse was in store.

Master stroke:
Sunil Gavaskar shares his experience

Sachin lost his father and had to go back to Mumbai for the funeral. It's difficult to say how much this affected the Indian team as a whole, but they played like a bunch of schoolboys and lost their next match against Zimbabwe rather comically after being on top right through the game.

So glaring were India's mistakes on the pitch that it prompted Gavaskar to call for a probe into India's pathetic show.

India were now in a desperate situation and they needed someone to rise to the occasion. Someone whom the other players could rally around. That man turned out to be Sachin. Pushed into a must-win situation against minnows Kenya, India turned to Sachin, who had returned to the fold after his mother

Rajani had urged him to respond to the nation's call. 'Your Father would have been more proud to see you doing your duty for the country. The Indian team needs you and you should be there,' his mother had urged, prompting Sachin to return to England in time for the Kenya match.

At Centurion Park, before Sachin got going in the 2003 World Cup

And what an impact he made straight away. It was a classic innings from the 'Little Master' who put his personal tragedy behind him to give his team a lifeline. After reaching his century Sachin just looked up at the heavens as if to say, 'This one is for you, Father'. With Rahul Dravid too scoring a hundred, India hit the winning road again. They, however, still needed to win their remaining two group matches to qualify for the Super Six.

Their next match was in Taunton against the reigning world champions, Sri Lanka. Dravid carried his super form into this

match as well and was the first to reach his half-century. But after that, the 'Bengal Tiger' took over. In the process, Sourav went past Kapil Dev's 175 not out, which till then was the highest individual score by an Indian in the World Cup. Sourav simply toyed with the Sri Lankan bowling in making a magnificent 183. Dravid notched up his second successive hundred and the duo added 318 runs for the second wicket. The result became a foregone conclusion, leaving India with the task of bearding the English lion in its own den in their final league encounter.

Like in 1983, England failed again in their objective to stop India. Sourav contributed a gritty 40 with the ball moving around considerably in heavy English conditions and later picked up three important wickets as well. This all-round show enabled him to pick up his second successive Man-of-the-Match award and India qualified for the Super Six stage in style. However, with South Africa and Zimbabwe also qualifying from the group it was always going to be a tall order for India.

Zimbabwe was infinitely better placed with six carry-over points from the league by virtue of their shock wins over the other two teams to qualify from its group—India and South Africa. The Proteas, too, had three points, having beaten India, but Azhar's team had no points to carry over. They were faced with the onerous task of beating all the three teams from the other group which had made the Super Six—Australia, Pakistan and New Zealand to qualify for the last-four stage.

India played their worst game against the Australians. Steve Waugh's team was on a roll after a stuttering start to their campaign. Waugh, the astute captain that he is, called upon his best bowler Glenn McGrath to get the best rival batsman out, through his column. McGrath obliged his skipper with the wickets of Brian Lara and Sachin. India were simply powerless to stop them.

Sourav picked up an injury in that game and missed an all-important clash against Pakistan. India played a great match and won it comfortably, thanks to a couple of wonderful spells by Venkatesh Prasad.

With just two points in their kitty, India were all but out of the tournament. They needed a miracle against the Kiwis in their last Super Six match. Sourav returned to the fold, but hardly made an impact and the Kiwis romped home by five wickets to make the semi-final.

Sourav with Sachin at a practice session

India's World Cup dream had been shattered, but Sourav came back from England having scored 379 runs in seven matches at an average of 54.14 with a big hundred and two MoM Awards.

Little did he know that four years down the line, he would be leading India in the 2003 World Cup in South Africa. Sourav become the fourth Indian skipper to lead the team in World Cup competition after Srinivas Venkataraghavan (1975 and 1979), Kapil Dev (1983 and 1987), Mohammed Azharuddin (1992, 1996 and 1999). More importantly, Sourav was ready for the job and his preparations were complete.

He had convinced Dravid to continue keeping the wickets and opened up the No. 7 slot for Mohammed Kaif. Javagal Srinath was back, bowling at his best with Zaheer Khan and Ashish Nehra providing adequate support. Sourav's only headache was in the spin department, for it was tough to choose between Harbhajan Singh and Anil Kumble. He chose to bite the bullet and opt for the younger and fitter Harbhajan and he himself sharing the fifth bowler's quota with Sachin, Sehwag and Yuvraj.

India began their campaign against the minnows Holland. For one Sourav decided to renew his opening partnership with Sachin and demoted Sehwag to No. 3. This decision came in for much criticism as Sehwag was the only Indian batsman to have tasted some success on their tour of New Zealand which had preceded the World Cup. Moreover, the Sachin-Sourav association did not click against Holland. It also failed against Australia.

Not only the skipper, but almost every member got the stick from the media as well as the fans for their spineless display that saw them score just 125 against the world champions. Fans in India went berserk. Stones were thrown at Kaif's house in Uttar Pradesh and effigies of our cricketers were burnt. Fans just refused to believe that the team was trying its best. Just about everyone had written off the Indian team but for the skipper himself. Sourav was

Analysing the situation with Arun Lal

BRITANNIA
WILLS
BRITANNIA

Facing page:
With Rahul Dravid, who would succeed him as captain, in Taunton in 1999

convinced that he had a great team under him which perhaps needed a bit of time to settle down.

India's third match was against Zimbabwe in Harare. There were serious security concerns in Zimbabwe and England even refused to travel to Harare and thus forefeited three important points. Indians, however, could not afford such luxury and travelled to Harare where Sachin opened with Sehwag and Sourav batted at No. 4. The Mumbai maestro made a masterly 81 to lift the morale of the team.

In the next match, both Sachin and Sourav got hundreds against newcomers, Namibia, in Pietermaritzburg. It was Sachin's fourth hundred in World Cup competition while it was Sourav's second. After two soft games, India faced a big challenge from England. India batted first and made a none-too-impressive 250, but Nehra bowled a superb spell to confirm India's place in Super Six. Nehra's six for 23 underlined his considerable talent yet again. He seemed to have toughened up mentally and bowled with rare fire and aggression in that match. Perhaps not used to bowling his entire quota of overs in one spell, he took ill and even threw up on the ground, but carried on gamely to finish his spell.

So, before the all-important match against Pakistan, India were already through to the next phase. But an India-Pakistan match is always much more than that. As Pakistan had never beaten India in a World Cup tie, India also had a record to protect.

Saeed Anwar has always been a dangerous customer, especially against India. Anwar lived up to this reputation once more, scoring a splendid century to lead Pakistan to a reasonably good total of 273. Sachin and Sehwag launched India's chase, but failed to provide the kind of spark that was required at the start of the innings. They added 53, but then Sehwag and Sourav fell in a heap to Waqar Younis to leave India in a state of great discomfort. Sensing this Sachin decided to attack Pakistan's bowling. And by the time he was through, there was nothing much left to do. Sachin missed his century by just two runs, but in terms of quality, his 98 would rank among his best efforts in one-day cricket.

Sanath Jayasuriya has a problem on his hands. Sourav looks at it

Unlike in 1999, India were in the Super Six with four precious points. And they had reason to believe that a semi-final spot was there for the taking as they only had to beat two of the following three teams: New Zealand, Sri Lanka and Kenya.

Sourav scored his third World Cup hundred against the Kenyans to lead India to victory. His detractors may dismiss his effort as 'a routine hundred' against minnows, but at one stage when India, chasing 226 for victory, were 24 for three, it had looked rather ominous. Sourav, in the company of Dravid and Yuvraj, settled the issue.

Sri Lankans rarely performed well outside the Emerald Isles. So, it was no surprise when they caved in without a fight against India. With Sachin and Sehwag adding 153 runs in a rollicking opening-wicket stand, the Sri Lankans had resigned themselves to chasing a big score. Tendulkar again missed a century, this time by three runs. Sehwag made 66 and Sourav contributed 48 in India's final tally of 292. Indian pacers rocked Sri Lanka with their pace and movement to bundle them out for 109. A semi-final spot was thus confirmed, but India still needed to set the record straight against the Kiwis, especially after suffering much at their hands in New Zealand just before the World Cup. Indian fast bowlers came into their own once more and bowled with sustained hostility and accuracy to bundle out New Zealand for 146.

Shane Bond, who had given Australia a taste of their own medicine in an earlier match, rocked India's top-order, removing Sachin, Sehwag and Sourav in quick succession, but with so few runs on the board, New Zealand skipper Stephen Fleming found his bowling resources stretched. Dravid and Kaif took full advantage of this to see India through.

As luck would have it, India were up against Kenya in the semi-final. Sourav hit his third hundred in the 2003 World Cup, a rare feat. It was enough to seal a berth in the final for his team. India was in a World Cup final after exactly 20 years.

They were up against the best team in the world who had progressed to the title-round without having lost a single match in the competition. A remarkable achievement, considering the fact that they had bowled the Indians out for a paltry 125 in the group league.

Indians, too, had not done too badly. Their only loss had come against Australia. Winning eight straight matches is no mean achievement in a tournament as big as the World Cup. It was, therefore, only fair that the final was being contested between the two best teams in the world.

After winning the toss on a cloudy morning, Sourav did not hesitate to put the Aussies in. His fast bowlers had been superb in the tournament. He simply wanted them to have a go at the Aussie top-order rather than asking his batsmen to face Glenn McGrath and Brett Lee in overcast conditions.

Zaheer Khan lost his cool early on and got into a verbal duel with the two Australian openers. But it didn't help India's cause. Skipper Ricky Ponting and Damien Martyn were ruthless on anything short of length and the three Indian fast bowlers gave away more than 200 runs. It left India with an onerous task of chasing 360 to win the World Cup a second time.

India had lost the match even before the chase. Sehwag batted beautifully and got some support from Dravid, but it was never going to be enough against a disciplined Australian attack. The Aussies retained the World Cup in style. The Indians, however, came back from South Africa with their heads held high. They were outplayed by Australia in the final, but they had lost to the best team in the world and their twenty-year dream remained unfulfilled.

Fit for a king:
at the gymnasium at
Eden Gardens

Dil bhi jeeta, aur series bhi

Truth, they say, is stranger than fiction. The myth is that every Indian cricket captain fantasises about leading a team to Pakistan. The truth is Indian captains, over the years, have generally dreaded the task, simply because Pakistan has proved to be a graveyard for them ever since we started playing Test match cricket in 1932. India, of course, played their first Test against Pakistan in 1952.

Before Sourav Ganguly's Team India returned victorious from Pakistan in 2004, no Indian team had even won a single Test across the border. Many Indian skippers in the past had gone to Pakistan with victory on their minds, but all of them came back empty-handed. Let alone winning a series, till 2004, India had

With one of his many finds—Irfan Pathan

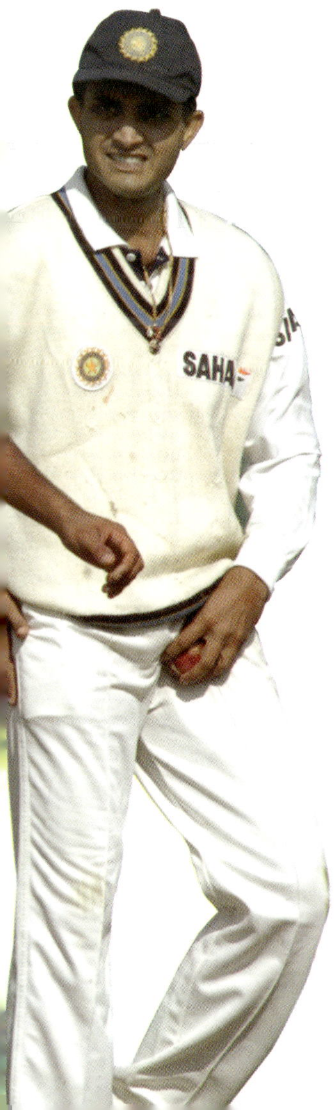

never even won a single Test match in Pakistan under any of those stalwarts.

These captains also lost their jobs after each unsuccessful sojourn. No captain has survived the axe. Not even Krishnamachari Srikkanth, the only Indian skipper to have returned from Pakistan after drawing the series there in 1989, thanks to Sanjay Manjrekar, who scored more than 500 runs in the four Tests India played there.

Srikkanth had to make way for Mohammed Azharuddin because of his own pathetic form during the series as well as the Indian cricket board's internal politics. Srikkanth had even fought hard for Azhar's inclusion in the squad for the Pakistan tour. The Hyderabadi stylist was going through a lean patch. Having succeeded in his endeavour, Srikkanth, however, could not find a place for Azhar in the first Test. But when Raman Lamba picked up an injury, Azhar made the team for the second Test. A few tips from Pakistan's batting legend Zaheer Abbas worked wonders for Azhar, who even ended up scoring a century. Zaheer, who had analysed Azhar's problem, had suggested a slight change in Azhar's grip and the result was there for everyone to see.

When the team came back to India, Raj Singh called up Azhar with the captaincy offer with his now famous quote: *'Miya kaptaan banoge*?'. A bewildered Azhar accepted the promotion gratefully and poor Srikkanth was dropped from the Test team.

It was no surprise really because top Indian cricketers in the past had their careers cut short after each Pakistan tour. After the famous 1978 'Revival Series', the Indian spinners had, more or less, met with the same fate. Having been put to the sword by the marauding blades of Zaheer and Javed Miandad, the famous spin troika of Bishen Singh Bedi, Erapalli Prasanna and Bhagwat Chandrasekhar suffered an irreversible loss of form. Prasanna and Chandrasekhar never played another match after coming back from the tour, while Bedi, who was the skipper, barely lasted a couple of series after that.

With Greg and Judy Chappell in Adelaide after Sourav's 144 in Brisbane

Facing page:
A cool session in the pool

The same thing happened after the 1982-83 series when India lost the six-Test series 3-0. Sunil Gavaskar lost the captaincy and his brother-in-law Gundappa Viswanath was axed from the side. The 1989 series was special because 16-year-old Sachin Tendulkar had made his Test debut on this tour. Little did Sachin know at that time that on India's next tour of Pakistan (in 2004) he would be the sole survivor from the 1989 squad.

So, it was never going to be easy for Sourav's team which had settled down quite well under him, but had little or no experience of playing in Pakistan. To make matters worse, Harbhajan Singh, India's main wicket-taking hope, had to pull out injured.

The 2004 tour of Pakistan was a historic one for more reasons than one. The two rivals had not played much cricket on each other's soil for the past 15 years and the Kargil War had soured relations between the two countries. Although Indian and Pakistani cricketers have always enjoyed a healthy relationship, the political tension between the two countries continues to simmer over various issues ranging from Kashmir to terrorism. Indo-Pak cricket has always been played in the backdrop of the three wars that the two nations have fought since gaining independence in 1947.

Fanatics have chosen to play on these sentiments by labelling an innocuous game of cricket between the two teams as jihad (religious struggle), as if it were the 'holy' duty of the likes of Imran Khan, Javed Miandad, Inzamam-ul Haq, Sunil Gavaskar, Kapil Dev and Sachin Tendulkar to annihilate the opposition on a cricket pitch. Failures have been rarely tolerated in Indo-Pak cricket. Perhaps that's what adds spice to such encounters, which have replaced the Ashes as the No. 1 rivalry in the 'Gentleman's Game'.

No India-Pakistan game is devoid of drama or intrigue. One of the most tension-filled India-Pakistan match in recent times was witnessed in the 2003 World Cup in South Africa. India won that group-league match to keep their unbeaten record against Pakistan in World Cup competition intact, but there was simmering tension between the traditional rivals who were under extreme pressure to win the game.

Pakistan had run up a score of 273 after they had won the toss. According to sources close to both the teams, during the break, Harbhajan Singh, Yousuf Youhana (now Mohammed Yousuf) and Shahid Afridi were involved in a brawl that fortunately didn't go out of hand. And the organisers had arranged for both the teams to have lunch together. Apparently, while having their food, Yousuf and Afridi had taunted Harbhajan, who was not playing the match. Not one to take things lying down, Harbhajan returned the verbal volley. He was ably assisted in his endeavour by the likes of Yuvraj Singh, Zaheer Khan and Ashish Nehra. The senior players of both sides intervened to diffuse a potentially volatile situation. One can recall numerous such instances over the years.

Politicians on both sides of the borders have been quick to realise the importance of cricket in Indo-Pak relations. So you have had periods of lull with both nations

SAHARA
SAHARA
SAHARA
ZULFI

Facing page:
The leader leads

refusing to play on each other's soil, but have readily crossed swords with each other on so-called 'neutral' venues for a few dollars more.

In 2004, when India's tour of Pakistan was okayed by the Indian government led by Prime Minister Atal Behari Vajpayee, the message was loud and clear: Diplomacy would be an equal partner with cricket right through the series. This point was underlined by Mr Vajpayee himself during a high tea hosted by him for the Indian cricketers prior to the tour. What the Prime Minister told them has, of course, become one of the most quotable quotes in India's cricket history. *'Match bhi jeetiye aur dil bhi* (Win matches as well as hearts)' was the message from the charismatic leader.

The Indian cricketers were received with warmth when they crossed the Wagah border. There has never been any animosity towards cricketers of either country, no matter how tense the diplomatic ties have been. Sachin Tendulkar has always been as popular in Pakistan as Wasim Akram in India.

Indians were clearly moved by the bonhomie and the hospitality, but to their credit, they didn't let themselves be swept off their feet. They, perhaps, consciously wanted to avoid the fate of the Indian team that had toured South Africa in 1992-93. The Proteas were hosting a home series for the first time after 22 years and they had gone out of their way to make the Indian team feel at home. So moved were the Indian cricketers by the endless receptions that they could not focus on their game and ended up losing the series badly. Sourav's team was different, for, here was a side dying to do well in Pakistan and were all charged up.

The skipper made his stand clear during his first official press conference in Pakistan—he meant business. When Pakistani journalists asked him how his team would cope with the 'Rawalpindi Express (Shoaib Akhtar)' Sourav, displaying admirable wit, had quipped: 'We will derail the Rawalpindi Express.' This 'front-footed drive' by the Indian skipper made

him a great hit among Pakistanis who love to compete against tough opponents. Sourav was ready to take the fight right up to the hosts' dressing-room and at the same time win the hearts of the Pakistanis.

Facing page: Sourav Ganguly: confidence personified

Rising ball—a problem? Says who?

India began the one-day series in style by winning a thriller. Pakistan, chasing India's mammoth tally of 349, almost pulled off a miraculous victory, with Inzamam-ul Haq scoring a scintillating hundred. Moin Khan failed to do to Ashish Nehra what Javed Miandad had done to Chetan Sharma in Sharjah almost 20 years ago and Pakistan lost by a narrow margin of just five runs.

The hosts, however, came roaring back in the series by winning the next two games. In the second game at Rawalpindi, it was India's chance to chase a big score as Pakistan piled up 329 in their allotted overs. The Indian charge was led by Sachin Tendulkar who scored a splendid 141 off 135 balls, but the lower order could not sustain the momentum and India fell short by 12 runs.

India suffered a batting failure in the third match and could manage to put up just 244 runs on the board. Young Pakistani opener Yaseer Hamid led the charge and Pakistan looked in control. However, an expected middle-order collapse put Pakistan in a spot of bother at 173 for six in 35 overs. Abdul Razzaq and Moin Khan then launched a counter-offensive to which India had no answer.

In the fourth match, Dravid and Kaif came to India's rescue and helped to level the series 2-2, turning the last match into a final of sorts. Realising that there was a good chance to win the series, Sourav rallied his troops, saying, 'If we can draw level, we can win the series as well'.

And the Indians did it in style, winning by a convincing margin of 40 runs. They made a bit of history in the bargain. No Indian team had won even a one-day series in Pakistan earlier. However, there was a downside to this great achievement as Sourav had picked up an injury during the last match.

'The injury could not have come at a worse time for me as I desperately wanted to play in the Test series. I did not get a big score in the ODIs, but as a batsman, I knew that I was in good nick. I was getting a start, but either a rash stroke or a momentary lapse in concentration was doing me in. I was, therefore confident that I would be able to turn it around in the Tests. However, the back injury I suffered during fielding in the final ODI, forced me to sit out the first Test match,' Sourav recollected.

The mood in the Indian camp was upbeat. Having beaten Pakistan, in Pakistan, in a one day series, was a definite high, but the Men in Blue wanted more. What gave India added confidence was their wonderful performance in the Test series in Australia few months back.

However, they refused to get carried away being aware that the loss of the ODI series on their home soil would spur Inzy and his boys to raise their game.

Sourav did not play the first Test, but was there with the team in Multan. Virender Sehwag begun the Test series in a way only he can. In Melbourne, he had failed to reach his double-hundred because his attempted six had failed to clear the boundary ropes and he was caught in the deep. In Multan, he rode his luck merrily. He was dropped on several occasions by butter-fingered Pakistani fieldsmen, but this time he was not to be denied. He scaled one peak after another and broke all individual batting records to become the first Indian batsman to register a triple-hundred.

Sachin, on 194, was coasting to his double-century when Dravid decided to declare the Indian innings abruptly much to the surprise of all and sundry, including the 'Little Master' himself. India coach John Wright, in his book, has detailed the tense atmosphere in the Indian dressing room and the cold relations between Dravid and Sachin following the declaration. Sachin was so aggrieved by that inexplicable gesture of his captain that for the first time in his career he burst out at a press conference at the end of the day's play. He clearly stated that no instruction was sent to him to hurry up. This put Dravid under extreme pressure. However, peace returned to the Indian camp when we won

One more on the off side

the Test by an innings and 52 runs. Dravid had become the first Indian captain to win a Test on Pakistan soil and the whole of India rejoiced.

There was, however, no joy for Sourav, who decided to return home for treatment at this juncture. With their leader not in their midst and Pakistan going all out, India lost the second Test in Lahore by nine wickets. Pakistan unearthed a new pace-bowling hero in Umar Gul, who swung the ball appreciably on a green wicket and helpful conditions to skittle out India for 287. Only Yuvraj Singh could weather the Pakistan onslaught with a courageous 112. In reply, Pakistan piled up 489 with skipper Inzy and Imran Farhat scoring centuries. India managed just 241 in their second essay with only Sehwag (90) and Parthiv Patel (62 not out) putting up any resistance. Pakistan knocked off the required runs easily and the series was back on an even keel (1-1).

The final Test in Rawalpindi, thus turned into a decider and Sourav, having recovered from his injury, air-dashed back to Pakistan to join the action. The Indians were really charged up to win the series. Indian pace bowlers did a good job, first up by dismissing

Pakistan for 224. Laxmipathy Balaji, the most improved bowler on the tour, grabbed four wickets while Nehra and Pathan bagged two apiece to push Pakistan on to the back foot. Indian batsmen then piled up 600 runs to raise visions of a historic win. Dravid was the pick of the Indian batsmen. A stupendous 270 from his broad blade knocked the stuffing out of Pakistan after Sehwag and Sachin had failed. Sourav and Laxman chipped in with sparkling half-centuries to rub salt into Pakistan's wounds. Sourav made 77 and was looking good for a hundred when he again threw away his wicket. A hundred on Pakistan soil thus eluded him.

Faced with the task of saving the match, Pakistani batsmen panicked. Balaji and Kumble shared the spoils to make a dream come true for every Indian.

Facing page:
I love my India

A delicate touch to send the ball to the fine-leg boundary

Sourav's new Team India had now come into its own. It was a totally different side. In less than two year's time, India had drawn two away series against Australia and England, won a Test in the West Indies, Sri Lanka and Zimbabwe and now won a Test series in Pakistan.

And more, importantly, Indian cricketers had won Pakistani hearts, too.

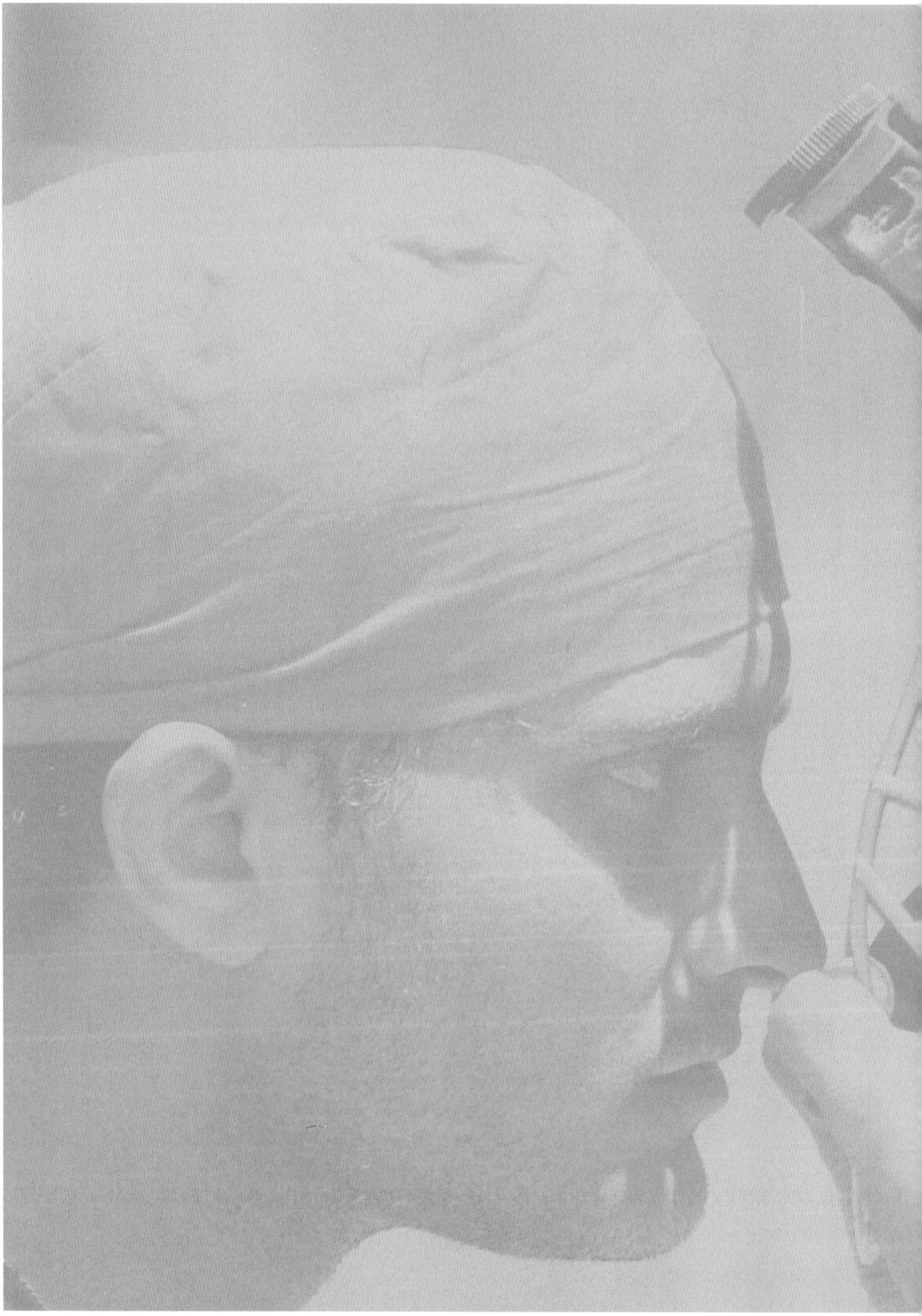

Passion in a blue shirt

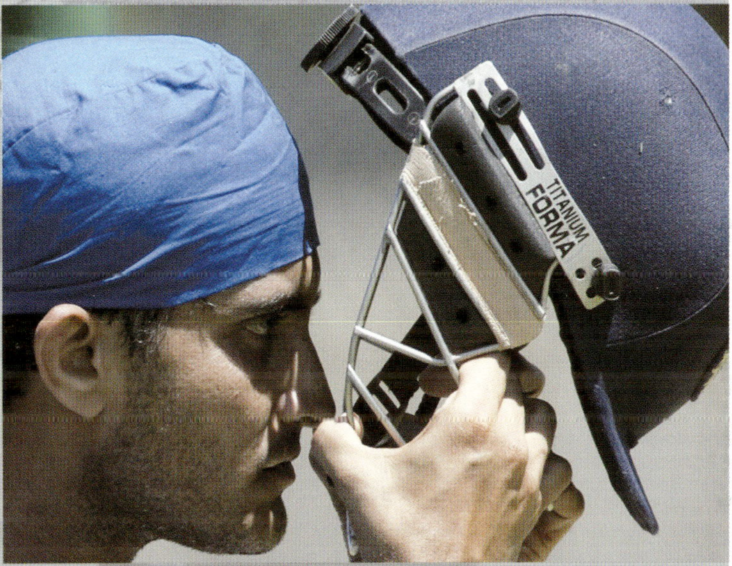

Lord's, July 13, 2002. Sourav Ganguly will never forget this date. It was on this day that his team notched up an improbable victory, beating England in the NatWest Series Final. Beginning with the 2000 ICC Champions Trophy in Nairobi, the Indian cricket team had reached the final of a tournament involving at least three teams on nine occasions. But each time they had failed to win the trophy, prompting the critics to dub them as chokers. So when the Nasser Hussain-led England set notched up 325 for five in their alotted 50 overs, another defeat looked imminent.

It was a good toss to win and Hussain showed no hesitation in choosing to bat first. India did meet with early success when Zaheer Khan castled Nick Knight for 14, but their hopes of making further inroads into the England innings were dashed by Marcus Trescothick and Nasser himself.

Facing page:
The Flagbearer—at the 2003 World Cup opening ceremony at Capetown

Below:
With Bengal Chief Minister Buddhadev Bhattacharjee and Lata Mangeshkar

England's two most experienced campaigners batted like champions and added 185 runs for the second wicket to push India on to the back foot. Hussain and Trescothick both hit centuries as the Indian attack wilted. Andrew Flintoff, who came

With Pankaj Roy at the CAB's annual prize distribution at the Eden Gardens.

in next, took full advantage of the situation and blasted a quickfire 40 off 32 balls to guide England to an apparently safe score.

India, which had gone into the match with just four frontline bowlers and seven batsmen, paid the price of dropping the in-form Ajit Agarkar. India's part-time bowlers—Sourav, Virender Sehwag and Yuvraj Singh—who shared the 10 overs among them, gave away 72 runs. India had a mountain to climb while chasing and their desperation showed when Sourav decided to go after the England bowling from the beginning. He edged a few, but fortunately for him the ball always landed on no-man's land. With Sehwag at the other end also in a punishing mood, the Indian openers added 106 in just 14.3 overs. They had laid the foundation for the chase and done so in style with the momentum in their favour. However with Sourav and Sehwag departing in successive overs and Dinesh Mongia and Rahul Dravid following suit, India's positive start had been nullified. And when Sachin Tendulkar, batting at No. 4, in this tournament, also departed after contributing just 14, India sank to 146 for five in 24 overs. Sachin's dismissal boosted England's morale and the players mobbed Ashley Giles who had managed to fox the master-batsman while pegging back his stumps. It looked a lost cause for India with all the big guns back in the pavilion. In the middle were two relatively inexperienced batsmen—Yuvraj and Kaif—who were expected only to delay the inevitable. Kaif and Yuvraj, however, had other ideas. Both these players had caught skipper Sourav's eyes a couple of years ago and since then he had nurtured them along. In fact, Sourav had to fight with the selectors in order to keep them in the squad, dismissing their inconsistency as youthful exuberance.

Sourav also bore the brunt of media criticism for including Kaif in this match as the seventh batsman. For this he had to persuade a reluctant Dravid to keep wickets. Experts were of the opinion that if six specialist batsmen cannot win a match, the seventh will hardly do. Dravid had made his displeasure known in no uncertain terms when Sourav had mooted the additional role for him, but agreed to don the big gloves in this match in the larger interests of the team. It was also during this series that Sourav had requested Sachin to bat at No. 4 instead of opening the innings, thereby fitting in Sehwag as an opener. The media had torn him apart for these radical changes, but each one of his 'experiments' bore fruit and skipper Sourav's stock rose considerably. Sachin scored two hundreds in the series. However, with the top order gone, it was left to the 'seventh wonder' Kaif to deliver something special in the company of Yuvraj, whose considerable talent had not yet found full expression.

What followed was straight from a fairy tale. Yuvraj and Kaif had added 121 runs for the sixth wicket to bring India back in the match. Just when it seemed that India were in with a shout, Yuvraj got carried away and was out for 69 to make it 267 for six. Kaif now had only the tail, comprising Harbhajan, Kumble, Zaheer Khan and Ashish Nehra, to bat with and get the 59 runs needed for victory. Yuvraj was so disappointed with his shot-selection that he had to literally drag himself out of the ground. In the dressing room he did not even take off his pads. Everyone was on the edge of their seats. Would Kaif be able to do it?

Most of the Indian players were on Lord's balcony chewing their fingernails. It was the same balcony where Kapil Dev Nikhanj and his 'devils' had made history on 25 June 1983 when India had won the World Cup.

It's a memory that no Indian cricket fan will ever forget. Will history repeat itself? Can the four tail-enders stay at the wicket to help Kaif knock off the remaining runs? Harbhajan, as usual, fought gallantly, scoring 15 valuable runs and in the process helped Kaif add

Facing Page:
The twirl at Lord's after the Natwest Trophy final

47 runs for the seventh wicket. With Kaif playing the innings of his life, it appeared that the Indians were through. But Flintoff had other ideas. The burly all-rounder bowled Harbhajan and also got rid of Kumble for a duck in the same over—the 48th of the innings. Twelve more were needed when Zaheer came to the crease. Kaif was determined not to expose the tail to the England and took it upon himself to make victory possible. Nine runs came off the penultimate over bowled by Darren Gough with Kaif hitting a boundary off the last ball. So, just two were needed off the last six ball to be bowled by Flintoff. The only problem was that Zaheer was on strike. The first two balls yielded no runs. Zaheer pushed the third ball to cover and ran for a single. A direct hit would have found Kaif, running to the danger-end short of the crease, but as luck would have it, the fielder missed and an overthrow resulted! India had scripted a historic win and a new Team India was born.

As TV cameras swung towards the Lord's balcony to capture the team's reaction, the world saw an overjoyed Sourav taking off his shirt and waving it wildly in an expression of raw emotion. It shocked the stiff upper-lipped British fans no end. It was not the done thing in what is considered to be a gentleman's game, but the Indians had no time to bother about all that after a miracle win.

As an overwhelmed Kaif was returning to the pavilion after a stupendous unbeaten 87 his skipper ran out and jumped straight into his lap. Yuvraj, still with his pads on, also ran out to hug Zaheer. The ensuing huddle, as others also joined in, told a new story. It was a triumph of team spirit fostered by new blood. Sourav had proved his critics wrong, one more time, as the seventh batsman had won the match for the team.

Unfortunately for Sourav, it was not India's great victory that made the headlines in the media, but his shirt-waving exercise. TV channels ran the footage of a bare-chested Sourav waving his India shirt on the Lord's balcony over and over again. SMS polls were commissioned, asking viewers to give their verdict on Sourav's seemingly ungentlemanly act.

omtex

At the Holy Thread ceremony with father Chandi Ganguly

Everybody seemed more concerned about the sanctity of the Lord's balcony rather than enjoying the spirited performances of the Indians. Sourav added a bit of fuel to the fire by declaring at the post-match press conference that his shirt-waving exercise was merely a tit-for-tat for Flintoff's similar deed in Mumbai when England had toured India in 2001. Sourav is known to wear his heart on his sleeves.

Those who know the Indian captain closely will tell you it was a spontaneous reaction from him. But try telling that to the Indian media, which was even more scathing in its criticism of their captain than the British press. 'It was not cricket. We often see it in soccer but not on a cricket field. What the Indian captain had done, disgraced a great game,' some of them opined. Sourav, however, was not bothered. There was no reason for him to be ashamed of his deed. If Flintoff could do it in Mumbai, the Mecca of Indian cricket, and get away with it, why should fingers be pointed at him.

Ironically, two years later when India went to play the ICC Champions Trophy in England, the curator of the Lord's cricket

A different partnership—this one for life

ground, Adam Chadwick, approached him for that very shirt he had waved from the 'hallowed' balcony. Sourav, of course, obliged. The shirt is on display now at the Lord's cricket museum. Chadwick later explained that by displaying it in the museum he wanted to portray the emotions that Sourav had experienced in those early moments of India's historic win. The historic Lord's match had at last found a rightful place in cricket's history.

Sourav has, since, gone on record saying that he will never repeat his shirt-waving exercise, but he has no regrets, for he remains a man who is driven by his emotions.

In real life, too Sourav remains a very passionate man—always willing to stand up for his beliefs if he thinks what he is doing is right. Take, for example, his marriage. He was in love with Dona when he was in his teens. Sourav's grandfather and Dona's grandfather were friends and business partners. The Gangulys and the Roys still live next to each other, but somewhere down the line relations became strained and a brick wall was built to separate the two houses much like we see in old Hindi movies.

But no wall or barrier has ever been able to separate two young people in love. Sourav and Dona were inseparable. They simply could not live without each other. They also knew that the elders in their families would not agree to their union. Frankly speaking, they had no choice but do what they did in the end.

Soon after returning from the historic tour of England in 1996, where Sourav emerged as the 'Lord of Lord's' following a century on his Test debut, he took the most important

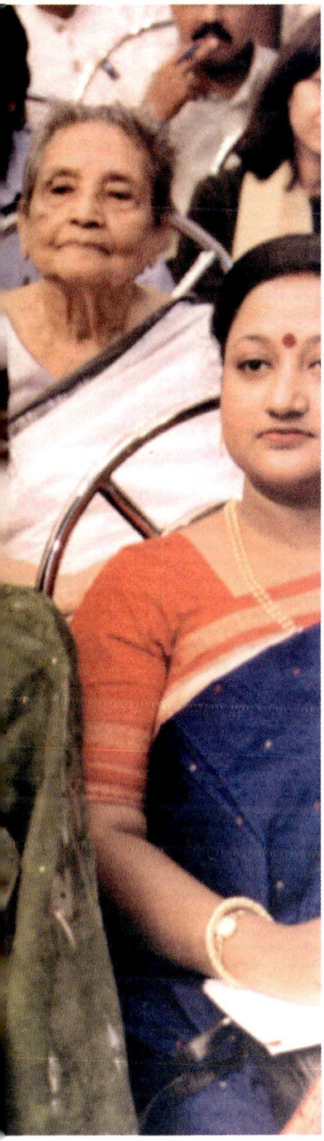

Mother Nirupa, wife Dona and Sourav's daughter Sana

decision of his life. Sourav's newfound confidence born out of success, perhaps prompted him to take the plunge. Dona was more than willing and the two love birds quietly got married. With some help from his friends, Sourav and Dona signed on the dotted line before a marriage registrar, who duly obliged.

It was too big a news to be kept under the wraps for long. A Kolkata daily broke the news first and others picked up the story and devoted columns of space to piece together the marriage of the decade. It came as a bolt from the blue for the two families. Sourav had gone into it with his eyes open and he stood firm. Despite their initial disapproval, both families got around to accepting the reality and Sourav and Dona settled down to a blissful matrimonial life. They made a lovely couple.

They now have a cute daughter, whom they have named Sana. Both Sourav and Dona avoid talking about those days of turmoil and are happy to have ridden out the storm. Says Dona, 'I like him for what he is. I know he is passionate about what he does. Otherwise, he is just a fun-loving boy-next-door. He loves to watch Hindi movies, *Phuchka* (*paani-puri*) is his favourite even now (mine too!). We had a particular *phuchkawala* from whom we used to have *phuchka*s every time we went out. We used to park our car at a distance and signal to him. He would bring the stuff over—*phuchka*s in a polythene bag and the tamarind water in a big *bhaar* (cup made of burnt clay). He never told anyone about his clients in the car. We really had fun in those days.' But what about now? Is he a caring husband? Dona says, 'Wherever he is, I know he will call me at least once in a day. Now, after Sana's birth, it's still the same.'

'His cricket assignments made him more responsible, I feel. But even today, if we ask him to go out with us whenever he is in town, he is always more than willing. In fact, he gets very excited about it.' Dona is a renowned Odissi dancer who made a lot of sacrifices for the sake of the family. Sourav also always encouraged her not to give up dancing. Dona has gone back to her second love in a big way. Deeksha-Manjari, her dance-school in south Kolkata is a well-known institution.

Bon appetit: Biriyani is a must for any family function

Chandi Ganguly, Sourav's father, was a former secretary of the Cricket Association of Bengal. He had played club cricket. In fact, the Gangulys own a cricket club called Barisha Sporting. Senior Ganguly has always been fond of the game and wanted both of his sons to pursue a career in cricket. His dream was fulfilled when both Snehasish and Sourav went on to play for Bengal and his youngest son became India's most successful skipper ever. 'I knew Maharaja (Sourav) was more fond of football but when he decided to take up cricket, I was glad. I knew he was talented. But what people do not know is the hard work he used to put in. I had built a gymnasium in one part of our residential complex so that both Raj (Snehasish) and Maharaja could work out there and keep up their fitness. I have seen them toiling. So I was not surprised when they succeeded.'

That Sourav is an emotional person is attested by his father as well. 'Maharaja was a bit emotional but possessed a very sharp

Brothers in arms

cricketing brain. When he was dropped after the Australia tour, he explained certain things to me and I knew he was maturing quickly. It was a bad experience for a youngster, but he only took the best out of it and banished the negatives. When he was recalled after four black years, his eyes told me that he was determined to succeed.'

'In his 10-year career he encountered a few problems. Initially, we used to get disturbed by it, but he would reassure us that everything would work out. I do not know from where he got this self-belief, but we are firm believers in destiny, so is he. And if he feels he has to do something, I know, he will do it without any regrets. When he was selected to lead the nation, we were proud but worried, too. It was hardly a good time to take up the captaincy. India had lost five consecutive Test matches, the match-fixing saga was on, but he simply relished the challenge. His honesty, coupled with a feverish desire to excel for his

Kookie Jar

country and passion for cricket enabled him to scale new peaks of success. I am really proud of him.'

There were numerous occasions on which his passion got him into trouble. Match referees often took him to task for a variety of reasons ranging from slow over-rate by his bowlers to over-appealing. He has been fined, warned and even banned, prompting some critics to question his aggressive instincts. He was being pulled up so often by match referees that a frustrated Sourav had once jokingly said that perhaps he should be dining regularly with them to avoid being penalised. But Sourav, being Sourav, didn't change. And thank God for that. He explained: 'What I do is for the team. If I appeal for a wicket I genuinely believe the batsman is out. Generally I come to bowl

Above:
A cake for 10,000 runs

Left:
One for the family album— in his Glamorgan apartment

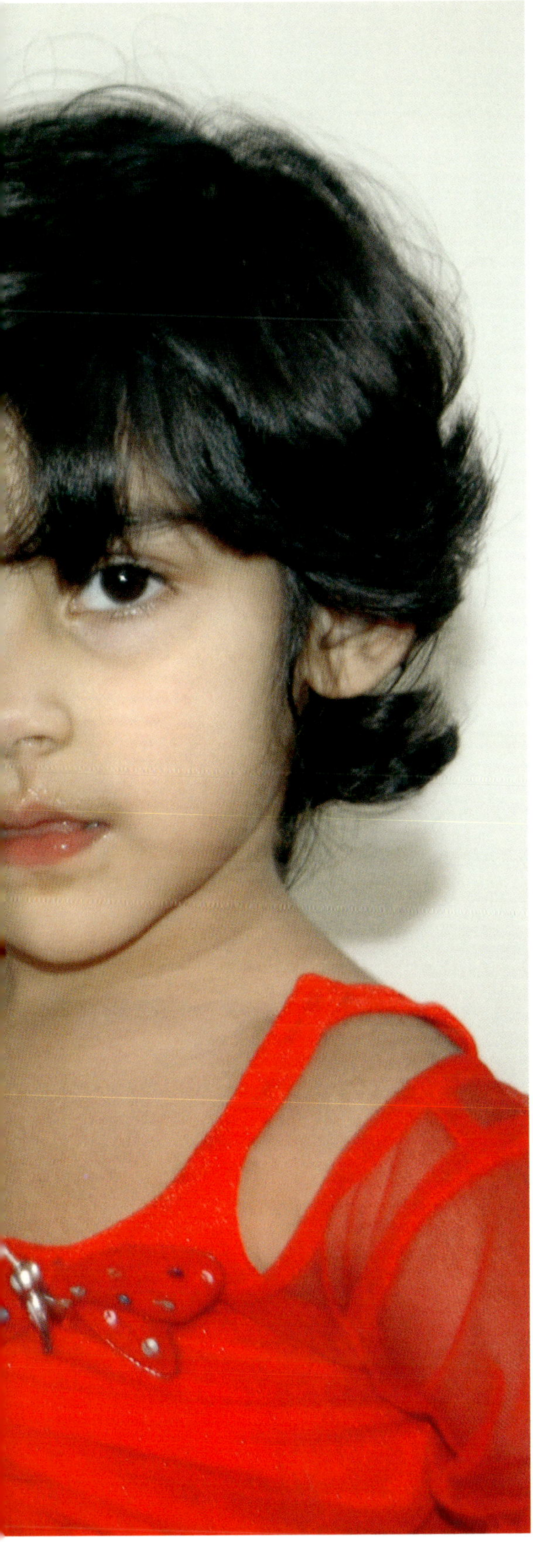

when we desperately need a wicket. So, an lbw-appeal may sound a bit louder, I cannot help that.

'People talk about our bowlers not completing overs in time. It might have happened on a few occasions, but at times we had genuine reasons for the delay. Like at the Eden one-dayer against Pakistan, the ball had to be dried after each delivery and their opener Salman Butt was injured. He had to be treated on the ground and that took more time.

'In Pakistan, we had three pacers. It was so hot and humid that the players needed to get some water in to avoid dehydration.'

Experienced skippers from the sub-continent like Imran Khan and Arjuna Ranatunga have always been very vocal about ICC's policy of punishing skippers for slow over-rates. They were of the opinion that the skipper should not be held responsible for the bowlers' actions. They wanted this rule to be abolished. However, the ICC did not reconsider these factors and Sourav was repeatedly pulled up by match referees. But Sourav, being Sourav, didn't change. And thank God for that.

He still believes that the game should be played passionately. Perhaps that's why he remains the best skipper in Indian cricket history and, perhaps the most loved.

Daddy's girl, Sana

What a comeback!

SAHARA
SS

'Why does he wish to hang on when the writing is clear on the wall? Why doesn't he negotiate with the board and settle for a farewell game?'

That was the common refrain until the South African tour happened. Even after the national selectors picked him for the Test series on that fateful day in November, 2006 there were a few Doubting Thomases who felt it was inappropriate to have picked him for the battle on the hard and bouncy wickets. It would only expose the former India captain's frailties. It would have been better to bring him back for the eight one-dayers against the West Indies and Sri Lanka at home to bolster his chances ahead of the World Cup.

Facing page:
Sourav announces his comeback with an unbeaten half-century in the first Test at Capetown, South Africa

At the nets during the 2006 South Africa tour

He has proved the critics wrong. The mental strength and ambition shown by Sourav Ganguly have made everyone sit up and take notice. The fairy tale happenings in South Africa have led everyone to believe that he has the makings of a champion. If you have self-doubt or are short on confidence, talk to Sourav and he will definitely show you a way out. How fast things change!

He has proved that one cannot keep a man with qualities out for long. He had very little time to acclimatise to the conditions, but one doesn't need that if one has the experience of playing close to 400 international matches under one's belt.

From the moment he landed in Johannesburg, he knew it was not going to be easy. The dressing room atmosphere couldn't have been conducive, there would be people to harp on the slightest of mistakes, and above all, he would also have to contend with a lively attack that had announced their intentions ('a hot welcome' was what Graeme Smith had promised) well ahead of his arrival.

As luck would have it, he received a warm welcome after meeting the players in Potchefstroom for a three-day warm-up game. From coach Greg Chappell to captain Rahul Dravid, all made it a point to make him feel comfortable.

The results showed. A gritty 83 against a decent South Africa-A attack. The will to perform and make a mark for himself showed. The form was encourgaing. That he would be in the team for the first Test in Johannesburg was a mere formality.

In discussion with Sachin Tendulkar during the second Test in South Africa in 2006

Facing page: Keeping his eyes on the ball till the last moment

Yet he wasn't allowed to speak to the media in Potchefstroom. 'The situation was volatile for both of us. So the team management thought both of us shouldn't speak,' Chappell revealed later. But the coach also acknowledged that the comeback had been encouraging and it showed that Sourav had worked hard.

Things started to fall into place. It showed in his body language and he wasted no opportunity to impress upon the team management that he was striving for success. He worked hard at the nets even on off-days, he was regular with gym sessions and took a keen interest in team meetings and gave valuable suggestions.

Nothing could stop him from performing. Hits to his body and head, a broken grill on his helmet, sledging, chin-music, et al. It seemed like he was destined to perform. 'I'll play even with broken bones... I won't give up,' he once said during the tour.

The first Test couldn't have been less dramatic. Sourav's unbeaten 51 in Johannesburg proved crucial in India's historic win at the Wanderers. 'You are entering the lion's territory,' the announcement at the entrance to the visitors' dressing room will never be

Concentration has always been Sourav's strong point

missed. It seemed like Sourav had raided the lion's den. The innings showed his grit, determination and application, three elements that proved vital in his success.

The Durban wicket was more bouncy. The South Africans were more hungry after the reverse in the first Test and it was a matter of survival for them. They were ready to go to any length to achieve their goal. The stage was set for another hostile attack. Makhaya Ntini and Andre Nel made the most of the conditions as the hosts levelled the series.

The final Test was set to be entertaining. The visitors faltered in more favourable conditions to hand over the series to South Africa on a platter. But Sourav didn't fail. A 66 and 46 confirmed his form and sent another timely reminder to the national selectors. A pulled four off Ntini during the final Test will stand out as one of the most memorable shots of the series.

The series ended on a high for him—218 runs as he emerged the highest run-getter for India. What a way to make a comeback for a man who had been ignored since the away Test series versus Pakistan in February 2006.

Accolades flowed thick and fast. Sunil Gavaskar and Wasim Akram admitted it was a mistake to keep him out for nine months and only Indian cricket was the loser. Ravi Shastri felt he was a changed man and the performances proved he had worked hard in the domestic circuit to fine-tune himself for tougher international battles ahead.

Sourav himself admitted this comeback was tougher than 1996 during the England tour. The circumstances were different, he was not getting any younger and he had to constantly egg himself on to keep the motivation going. His approach showed he had matured as a human being, while his hunger for runs had not diminished one bit.

Bengal hasn't produced many cricketers of repute. Pankaj Roy and Sourav are the only ones who have made their mark on the international stage. I would be happy if this book inspired any of the promising players to make it big. Sourav's deeds, his never-say-die attitude, courage and fighting qualities should also serve as enough motivation.

His success is now part of folklore. Even if he felt the tension and pressure, he didn't show it. Like a true professional, he showed that he can deliver when it comes to the crunch.

It was 'Now or Never' for Sourav in South Africa. The Maharaja proved true to his name.

First among equals

Like any other young lad growing up in the City of Joy in the 1970s, Sourav was crazy about football. He was at his happiest kicking the ball around with his friends and classmates, until his father thrust a bat in his hand and irrevocably shaped the future of a man on whom destiny would always rest its benevolent hand. Not a natural left-hander to start with, Sourav gradually mastered the nuances of batting and began to score prolifically, so much so that he was picked to join the Indian team for the tri-series in Australia in 1991-92 when he was only 19 years old.

It wasn't a happy initiation for the teenager. He only played one match in the tournament, against West Indies in Brisbane, making three runs before being trapped leg before by Anderson Cummins. For the next four and a half years, he was steadfastly overlooked for national representation until he secured a Test call-up for the tour of England in the middle of 1996.

Sourav wasn't a popular pick at the time. The general consensus was that it wasn't just the weight of runs that had propelled him to the Test squad, a misconception stemming from the fact that few who made those remarks had actually seen him bat in domestic cricket. Sourav wasn't a shoo-in for the Test eleven; that much was apparent when he wasn't selected for the first Test. But when Navjot Singh Sidhu abandoned the team midway through the tour after a run-in with the team management, Sourav's Test debut came to a fruition at Lord's, the Home of Cricket.

Even before the match, neither skipper Mohammad Azharuddin nor coach Sandeep Patil was particularly gung-ho about the left-handed Kolkatan. Sourav calmed his nerves by picking up the wickets of Nasser Hussain and Graeme Hick with his medium-paced wobblers, then proceeded to put on an exhibition of top-quality batsmanship when India came out to bat in quest of England's 344.

Walking in at No. 3 with India on 25 for one, Sourav lit up the landscape with stunning strokes through the off-side. His effortless timing and great grace elicited gasps of appreciation from the normally subdued Lord's gathering, and convinced his teammates that he had earned his spurs in his own right, not because he had a godfather facilitating his entry into the national side. Patil later admitted to me that before the tour, he had not seen Sourav bat because he himself was in his early days as the team coach/cricket manager.

When Sourav was finally dismissed for 131, Azhar showed his class in no uncertain terms. The skipper who had been reluctant to field the rookie came down from the dressing room to receive the centurion at the entrance to the Long Room, and presented him on the spot with the expensive watch he had been wearing. To this day, it remains one of Sourav's most coveted possessions.

Sourav was keen not to be a one-Test wonder. To him, that would suggest failure, and add further grist to rumours that he didn't deserve to play for India. 'I want to be a match-winner for a long time for the country, not just be satisfied with one Test appearance,' he had told me then. The morning after his maiden century, Sourav was standing all by himself in the middle of the ground before the start of play, soaking in the atmosphere and reliving his glorious knock. Up walked Geoff Boycott to congratulate the youngster. Thus began a relationship that has grown stronger over time. Boycott was impressed with not just Sourav's clarity of thought but also his insights into the game.

It was also at Lord's that Rahul Dravid made his debut, and even though he missed out on a century by five runs, it was obvious that these two youngsters would serve Indian cricket for a long time alongside the established names such as Azhar and obviously Sachin Tendulkar. As if to show that their Lord's heroics were no flash in the pan, Sourav and Rahul were both among the runs in the next Test in Nottingham. Once again, a century eluded Rahul as he fell for 84, but there was no stopping Sourav. By now high on confidence, he matched Sachin stroke-for-stroke during a partnership of 255, scoring a sparkling 136 to cap what was personally a massively successful tour for him. It was the first of many massive associations between the two men, who formed one of the most feared opening combinations in 50-over international history, subsequently.

Looking ahead

Patil told me after the series that at Lord's, Sourav didn't look at all like he was making his debut. 'I hadn't seen much of his previously, but after he made runs in the tour game against Derbyshire, I knew the lad could bat. At Lord's, there was no indication that he was overawed either by history, the stage or the occasion. He batted like a seasoned pro; that came as a breath of fresh air. He was in the zone, and he didn't make the mistake of trying to copy or match the batsman at the other end.' The batsman at the other end during the double-hundred stand in Nottingham was no less impressed. 'Dada wasn't beaten even once,' Sachin gushed. 'It was wonderful to watch him from such close quarters.'

Success in one format doesn't guarantee similar results, or even a place in the playing unit, in another. Not long after the England tour, from which he returned to Kolkata to a hero's welcome, Sourav had an underwhelming tour of Toronto for the Sahara

Cup against Pakistan. He made only 23 runs in three matches. The following year, at the same venue in the same tournament against the same opponent, he won four man of the match awards and was named the man of the series. On the eve of one of the games, bored of sitting idly in the dressing room watching the rain come down, he asked me to accompany him to the middle of the ground. There, he told me, 'My destiny has always been such that when I fail at a ground or a tournament, I always bounce back strongly. I leave an indelible mark, and I feel that's what is going to happen this time too.' Prophetic words those, considering the impact he was to make as the series unfolded.

When the captaincy was conferred on him towards the early part of 2000 for the one-day series against South Africa, Sourav was both overawed and nervous. Sachin had just stepped down as skipper in the middle of the Test series, and when Sourav entered the Kochi dressing room for the first time as the leader, he cast his eye around and was daunted at the men amongst whom he was. Former skippers Sachin and Azhar, and established superstars Rahul and Anil Kumble. For a brief minute, he was racked by indecision, if not insecurity. Then, he realised that he wasn't the captain by default. Everyone now looked up to him to lead the way forward. Emboldened by that, he outlined the style of play he wanted the team to adopt. It was a break from the past, where the onus had been on avoiding defeat first in Test cricket, especially overseas, and then looking for victory. Sourav's game plan revolved around being positive and fearless. He was willing to take risks in the quest for victory, much like Virat Kohli would do a decade-and-a-half later, and for an inspired bunch of individuals who were smarting from sub-par performances overseas, that was music to the ears. It is no coincidence that India's rejuvenation as a touring side came when Sourav was in charge.

Also mindful of the treatment meted out to him when he first broke into the Indian team as a teenager in Australia, Sourav was determined to introduce a culture of welcomeness and inclusivity into the ranks. He was of the opinion that if a player was good enough to make it to the national side, he had the right to get chances to prove his credentials. A few failures at the start of his career should not define the player; that was something Sourav believed. As he instilled confidence and security among the young guns, the likes of Zaheer Khan, Yuvraj Singh, Mohammad Kaif and most notably Virender Sehwag started to flourish. Even though he was the captain, Sourav remained one of the boys. His doors were open to any and every one, and such was his nature that even the youngest and the newest member of the side wasn't afraid of pulling his leg or taking the mickey out of him. Sourav took such banter in his stride and never carried a grudge, no matter what the popular perception might be.

Sourav's career was at a crossroads soon after the ill-fated tour of Zimbabwe in 2005. After his well-publicised pow-wows with coach Greg Chappell, he was first stripped of the captaincy and then dropped from the team itself more than once. Time seemed to have passed him by when he wasn't selected for the tour of the West Indies in 2006, and again for the one-day series in South Africa a little later in the year. He flew down to New Delhi to meet Sharad Pawar, then the President of the BCCI, to press his claim and seek his support for his return to the national set-up. Little must he have realised at the time that a dozen or so years down the line, he himself would occupy the chair to which he was appealing!

His second coming as a cricketer was quintessential Sourav. It defined the kind of man he is, the fire that burns brightly within him, the fierce determination that doesn't allow him to back down in the face of a challenge, the 'I-will-show-you' guts and gumption that the entire world has witnessed for so many years. He arrived in Johannesburg to much scrutiny, and immediately fired his salvo with a match-winning half-century in the first Test that was complemented by the brilliant swing bowling of S. Sreesanth.

Now without the cares of captaincy and therefore able to internalize and worry only about his batting—rather than strategies, game plans, the performances and mindsets of his colleagues, bowling changes, field placements, et al.—Sourav found a second win. Four of his 16 hundreds came post 2007, in the last one-and-a-half years of his 12-year Test career. He realised his fierce ambition of making a Test hundred at his beloved Eden Gardens when he made 102 against Pakistan. In that same series, he ticked another massive box emphatically with his first, and only, double-hundred, a monumental 239 at the M. Chinnaswamy Stadium in Bengaluru.

India were without Sachin and future skipper Mahendra Singh Dhoni, and reeling at 61 for four in the first session with Yasir Arafat threatening to run riot, when Sourav was joined by fellow left-hander Yuvraj. For the next four hours, Pakistan were busy playing fetch as the fifth-wicket pair added an even 300. Yuvraj dominated the stand with a flowing 169, feeding off the confidence that Sourav's solidity at the other end transmitted.

By then, Sourav was less than a year away from retirement. He knew that his 100th Test was round the corner—the 239 in Bengaluru came in his 99th game—which was a massive milestone for someone who always wanted to be more than a one-match *aaya ram gaya ram*. I remember with fondness his pride and sense of achievement as he entered the Melbourne Cricket Ground for his 100th match on Boxing Day, 26 December, 2007. The Bangalore double-hundred, which he followed up with 91 in the second innings, had reignited his spark. In the first innings, he had batted for eight-and-a-half hours. The pitch on the first morning was damp, the ball was doing all sorts of things. Sourav was put through a searching examination by Arafat, Shoaib Akhtar and Mohammad Sami. 'I am not sure how I managed to get through that early phase,' he recalled during one of our numerous conversations. 'I was convinced that sooner or later, I would get a ball with my name on it. But I fought through that early phase, and then cashed in when the pitch eased out a little bit and the bowlers tired.

'I was so satisfied that so deep into my career, I could bat so long and pull my team through to safety. The first Test, the first century, will remain the most special one. Nothing can ever replace that. But the Bangalore double is right up there with the best, for the circumstances under which they came, and for the point which I proved to myself. I will cherish it almost as much as I do the 131 at Lord's.'

Sourav isn't a man for grand gestures, but he loves the small, good, heartfelt ones. He was delighted, if somewhat embarrassed, that Dhoni asked him to lead the team for a brief period during his final moments at the Test in Nagpur in November 2008. For a lot of the players, Sourav was still the skipper, more than three years after last holding that role. Sourav obliged Dhoni by taking charge for a while before handing the reins back to the man who would subsequently take India to the No. 1 Test ranking.

While Sourav and cricket are inextricably intertwined in a love affair for the ages, he isn't just about cricket, though. For all his superstar status, he is still the boy-next-door in Kolkata, especially during Durga Puja and other festivals. He is a regular at the pandals, he plays the *dhaak* and *dhunuchi-naach* with abandon just like the average Joe. He makes time to interact on a personal level with the people gathered there, fusing his natural charm with a sense of the occasion. During those times, it is hard to believe that this man is one of the biggest celebrities in the country.

Football too continues to remain his great love, and he is emotionally invested in ATK, the ISL team from Kolkata previously known as Atletico de Kolkata when it was also co-owned by Spanish La Liga club Atletico Madrid. Whenever he can, he makes it a point to watch ATK in action at the ground. When he can't physically make it, he keeps tabs on their progress through any and all means, and his daughter Sana is invariably present at all of ATK's home matches, at the Salt Lake Stadium. Sana and her mother Dona are also mad about football, and in December 2018, Sourav, Dona and Sana made a trip to Nou Camp, Barcelona's home ground, where he was presented with an FC Barcelona jersey with 'Dada 99' emblazoned at the back. Alongside the watch gifted by Azhar, this occupies pride of place in his overflowing cabinet of trophies and memorabilia.

Ready for new challenges

The Boss

Sourav Ganguly's last-minute elevation as the President of the Board of Control for Cricket in India might have caught many by surprise, but to those of us who have known him for a long time, it was anything but that. It is not as if Sourav nurtured great ambitions to take the short route to the post, but he has always been more than just a player. Sourav has never believed in being second-best, not when he started off as a batsman, not when he made his debut as captain, and certainly not when he assumed the role of the joint secretary of the Cricket Association of Bengal in his maiden capacity as a cricket administrator.

Sourav has seldom sat back and waited for things to happen. Instead, like he did with the Indian team when he changed the mindset and placed his faith in young charges to go with established superstars, he was also extremely proactive when he became the CAB president after the sad demise of Mr Jagmohan Dalmiya. One of the things that rankled him was that despite the iconic nature of the venue, the Eden Gardens was witness to several washouts despite a good drainage system because the sun hardly shone on the ground properly, given the manner of the stadium's construction. Immediately after taking charge, he imported tarpaulin covers from London to ensure that the entire outfield was covered in the event of rain. What this meant was that once the rain stopped, the ground staff could then swing into action and ensure that the mopping up operations went on at full tilt. The covers across the circumference of the outfield ensured that play could start not long after the rain stopped. The wisdom of his call to have the entire ground covered has become obvious more than once in the last three seasons.

Even during his captaincy days, Sourav placed a great deal of faith in fast bowling. History is repeating itself now with Virat Kohli riding on the embarrassment of pace riches at his disposal to make India a strong force not just at home, like in the past, but even overseas. In another far-reaching move, Sourav was responsible for a change in the nature of the Eden surface, panned previously for being slow and low. There is greater bounce and pace off the pitch now, and more assistance for the quicker bowlers in the country in Kolkata than anywhere else in the world. It should not

Taking over the boss's chair

be a surprise to anyone if that were to become the norm across the country.

As the head of the BCCI's technical committee, Sourav was instrumental in introducing India to pink-ball, day-night cricket in first-class cricket in the form of the Duleep Trophy. He is of the firm conviction that in order to bring people in for Test matches, it is imperative to have day-night Tests so that fans can come over and watch matches either after a day in office or at school. It is in the natural scheme of things that, not long after he became the board president, he cracked the whip and reinvigorated the push for day-night Tests.

All of these merely go to substantiate the fact that Sourav doesn't allow the grass to grow under his feet, that he is not into administration merely to embellish his CV. One of the first steps he took after becoming the BCCI boss was to announce that he would pay greater attention to first-class cricket, and to cricketers who cut their teeth at the domestic level. It's been a decade and more since the remuneration for first-class cricketers was last revised. In a country where, on an average, there are nearly 1,000 first-class cricketers, only 11 can play for the national side at any given time. The others need the security that they can still make a career out of playing the sport even if, for some reason or the other, they are unable to make the next step up to the international grade. The move to get state associations to offer contracts to players, along the lines of the central contract the BCCI gives to the national stars, is not just welcome but much needed because it can allay the fears of those aspiring to play for India and allow them to go about their business without the gremlins of self-doubt and insecurity gnawing at their mental innards.

The manner in which he handled the threat of Bangladesh not being able to send a full side to India in November following a players' strike in protest against various steps advocated by the Bangladesh Cricket Board (BCB) also speaks to his diplomatic and persuasive skills. Again stepping in early and not waiting for the issue to escalate, he got in touch with his counterparts with the

BCB and helped resolve a problem that could have snowballed into a major sore point in relations between the two boards, and between the Bangladesh players and their governing body. Another tick in the box for Sourav, who has been equally on the front foot whilst reaching out to the various managers in the BCCI to have a greater understanding of how things function.

Among his early pronouncements has also been a desire to address the vexatious conflict of interest issue that threatens to rob Indian cricket of the services of some of its most accomplished and wise cricketing heads. Sourav himself had been caught up in the conflict conundrum which didn't please him one bit. He understands that the expertise of a majority of the past cricketers revolves around cricket. Post-retirement, if they make a livelihood out of coaching, commentary, media work of other nature or by becoming mentors in the Indian Premier League, then that is but natural. To expect them to give up everything and slot into honorary roles within the BCCI in an era of professionalism and commonsense is both naïve and silly. Sourav will leave no stone unturned in his desire to requisition the services of his erstwhile colleagues and several other luminaries of the past, because if Indian cricket is to remain vibrant and successful for a long period of time, then it will need the expertise and inputs of players from across eras and spectra.

Seeking to assuage doubts over his future relationship with head coach Ravi Shastri, Sourav has made all the right noises on that front too. In one of the first episodes of *Dadagiri,* the hugely popular Bengali reality show on Zee Bangla, one of the participants,Tollywood actor called Kanchan Mallik threw a left-field question to him about the continued status of Shastri as the coach. Taken aback by the unexpected query on such a platform, it didn't take Sourav long to compose himself and point out that India have had a fantastic run under Virat and Ravi. Sourav has lived by the motto of learn from the past, live in the present and plan for the future. No matter what might have transpired between Ravi and him in the past, it is unlikely to play a part in Sourav's decision-making because he has always had the best interests of Indian cricket at heart, and he has too much class to indulge in pettiness and needless mud-slinging.

It was also big of Ravi to seek to bury past differences with his one-time India teammate and look forward to the future, where the paths of the two men are certain to cross quite regularly. Himself a former India captain, Ravi waited for Sourav to officially take charge as BCCI head on 23 October. The following day, through a text, he sent him a congratulatory message. Later on, in an interview to a newspaper, Ravi said, 'My heartiest congratulations to Sourav for taking over as the BCCI president. His appointment is an indication that Indian cricket is moving in the right direction. He's always been a natural leader. When someone like him—who already dipped his feet into cricket administration four or five years ago—takes over as president of the BCCI, it's a win-win for Indian cricket. These are difficult times for the Board and there's a lot of work to do to bring BCCI back on the path of glory. I wish him all the best in his stint.'

As things stand now, Sourav will only be the Board president for 10 months or so, after which the cooling off period, which is now in existence, will kick in. But the limited duration isn't something that bothers or daunts him. 'It's not about whether I am going to be the president for 10 months or more,' he made an open statement, 'It's all about what you can do to leave Indian cricket in a better place than when you assumed office. It's a huge honour for me that the members of the BCCI have placed so much faith in me and asked me to be the president. It's up to me now to make sure that I live up to the expectations of so many.'

A lot of those expectations stem from the fact that Sourav is the first big-name cricketer to be elected Board president in his own right. Agreed, the Maharaja of Vizianagaram was the BCCI chief more than 65 years back, but we all know how and why that elevation came about. A few years back, Shivlal Yadav and Sunil Gavaskar were temporarily elevated to that status by the Supreme Court. Sourav, however, remains the biggest name to be elected to that position, and because he played more than

'It is not enough to just dream'

100 Tests for the country and was a fantastic captain to boot, people will expect more from him.

In many ways, this is the coming to reality of an unfulfilled dream. His late father, Chandidas, was the secretary at CAB, so officialdom is something that runs in his blood. Recently, at a felicitation function by the CAB to celebrate Sourav becoming the BCCI president, VVS Laxman spoke about his early interactions with Sourav the administrator. 'It was a shock to the system to see Sourav sitting in a small room at the CAB office, tending to files and going about his duties as an administrator. It was also suggestive of the fact that Sourav took his responsibilities very seriously, that he wasn't merely the titular joint secretary of the association,' Laxman said at the event.

At the CAB, insiders are clear that Sourav was cut out for the three Ps—President of the CAB, President of the BCCI and President/Chairman of the International Cricket Council. Two of those three Ps are out of the way. Destiny will decide if the third P also eventuates at some stage in the future.

In agreeing to become the head honcho of the Indian board, Sourav has had to make numerous sacrifices, plenty of them with financial implications. It's commendable that he has made those calls, because he realizes that it is imperative for him to hold sway as President for cricketers as a community to be respected. He has always been his own man, and it was no surprise to see that in his very first official interaction with the media after his formal coronation, he came wearing the India blazer he received ahead of the 2003 World Cup in South Africa. It shows how meticulous and particular he is in the way he carries himself, in the signal he sends to the millions keenly following his every move.

'Everyone has a dream,' Sourav said recently, 'but it is not enough to just dream. You must have the credibility, the intellect and the desire to reach the top. And once you are there, you must chart out the pathway and nourish structures so that the way forward for those who are coming in becomes that much clearer and easier.'

Among the many roles he has had to shun since 23 October is the mentorship of Delhi Capitals in the Indian Premier League. In their previous avatar as Delhi Daredevils, the franchise had struggled to make an impression despite often possessing big names. Sourav wove his magic there too, convincing the management to invest strongly in youth and forging a strong connection with the Indian players in the squad. Sometimes, his decisions were not on the same page as those of Ricky Ponting, the coach. But through logic and rationale, he brought Ponting around to see his points of view. It is no coincidence that the Capitals made it to the play-offs last season by finishing third on the points table by winning nine of their 14 games. Sourav won't be around in an official capacity with the franchise going forward, but the culture he has shaped within the squad should serve them well when the next season of the tournament begins.

While he has abdicated all his other responsibilities, the one thing Sourav is unlikely to give up is *Dadagiri*. It's a show that is very dear to his heart, and it has attained such peaks of popularity that it is impossible to translate that into words. *Dadagiri* is Sourav's release, in many ways. It frees him up from all the tensions and stresses, and his spontaneity and enjoyment of his role in making it a top-notch show must be seen to be believed. The fluency with which he connects with the participants, the felicity with which he puts them at ease, and his banter with the audience brings out the natural showman in Sourav Ganguly.

There is plenty on Sourav's plate as he takes guard in his new avatar. Among them is returning India's primacy within the ICC. Due to various reasons, despite their massive superiority on the field and the huge chunk of revenue that they contribute to the ICC's coffers, India have been receiving step-motherly treatment from the world governing body of late. Sourav won't take that lying down. Given his experience of playing for so long, and with his administrative skills polished after five years in that capacity, Sourav is in the unique position of arguing from both points of view with equal skill and authority.

An exciting new chapter lies ahead not just of Sourav Ganguly, but also Indian and—by extension—world cricket. Seldom has the election as board president of a national cricket body evoked as much attention and anticipation as this one. And if his past record is anything to go by, Sourav will most certainly not disappoint this time either. It should be one fascinating, thrill-a-minute ride.

Statistics

Overall—Batting, Bowling & Fielding													
	Mat	Inn	No	Runs	HS	Ave	SR	100	50	Ct	Wkts	BB	BAvg
ODIs	311	300	23	11363	183	41.02	73.70	22	72	100	100	5/16	38.49
Tests	113	188	17	7212	239	42.17	51.25	16	35	71	32	3/28	52.53
1st Class	254	399	44	15687	239	44.18		33	89	168	167	6/46	36.52
List A	437	421	43	15622	183	41.32		31	97	131	171	5/16	38.86
T 20	77	73	4	1726	91	25.01	107.00	0	8	28	29	3/27	26.06

Indian Captains in Test Cricket							
Captains	Tests	Won	Lost	Drawn	Tied	Win%	Away wins
Virat Kohli	51	31	10	10	0	60.78	13
MS Dhoni	60	27	18	15	0	45.00	06
Sourav Ganguly	49	21	13	15	0	42.85	11
Mohd Azharuddin	47	14	14	19	0	29.68	01
Sunil Gavaskar	47	09	08	30	0	19.08	03
MAK Pataudi	40	09	19	12	0	22.50	03
Kapil Dev	34	04	07	22	1	11.76	02
Rahul Dravid	25	08	06	11	0	32.00	03
Sachin Tendulkar	25	04	09	12	0	16.00	00
Bishen Singh Bedi	22	06	11	05	0	27.27	03
Ajit Wadekar	16	04	04	08	0	25.00	02

Indian Captains in One Day Internationals					
Captains	Mat	Won	Lost	Tied	NR
MS Dhoni	200	110	74	05	11
Mohd Azharuddin	174	90	76	02	06
Sourav Ganguly	146	76	65	00	05
Virat Kohli	80	58	19	01	02
Rahul Dravid	79	42	33	00	04
Kapil Dev	74	39	33	00	02
Sachin Tendulkar	73	23	43	01	06

One Day Captains—All Time					
Captains	Mat	Won	Lost	Tied	NR
RT Ponting (Aus/ICC)	230	165	51	2	12
SP Fleming (NZ)	218	98	106	1	13
MS Dhoni (India)	200	110	74	5	11
A Ranatunga (SL)	193	89	95	1	8
AR Border (Aus)	178	107	67	1	3
M Azharuddin (India)	174	90	76	2	6
GC Smith (Afr/SA)	150	92	51	1	6
SC Ganguly (Asia/India)	147	76	66	0	5
Imran Khan (Pak)	139	75	59	1	4
WJ Cronje (SA)	138	99	35	1	3
DPMD Jayawardene (Asia/SL)	129	71	49	1	8
BC Lara (WI)	125	59	59	0	7
ST Jayasuriya (SL)	118	66	47	2	3

Test Captains—All Time					
Captains	Mat	Won	Lost	Tied	Drawn
GC Smith (ICC/SA)	109	53	29	0	27
AR Border (Aus)	93	32	22	1	38
SP Fleming (NZ)	80	28	27	0	25
RT Ponting (Aus)	77	48	16	0	25
CH Lloyd (WI)	74	36	12	0	26
MS Dhoni (India)	60	27	18	0	15
AN Cook (Eng)	59	24	22	0	13
SR Waugh (Aus)	57	41	9	0	7
Misbah-ul-Haq (Pak)	56	26	19	0	11
A Ranatunga (SL)	56	12	19	0	25
MA Atherton (Eng)	54	13	21	0	20
WJ Cronje (SA)	53	27	11	0	15
Virat Kohli (India)	51	31	10	0	10
MP Vaughan (Eng)	51	26	11	0	14
IVA Richards (WI)	50	27	8	0	15
AJ Strauss (Eng)	50	24	11	0	15
MA Taylor (Aus)	50	26	13	0	11
SC Ganguly (India)	49	21	13	0	15
GS Chappell (Aus)	48	21	13	0	14
Imran Khan (Pak)	48	14	8	0	26
M Azharuddin (India)	47	14	14	0	19
SM Gavaskar (India)	47	9	8	0	30
BC Lara (WI)	47	10	26	0	11
N Hussain (Eng)	45	17	15	0	13

Sourav: Career ODIs											
	Mat	I	NO	Runs	HS1	HS2	HS3	Ave	100	50	0
overall	311	300	23	11363	183	153*	144	41.02	22	72	14

Runs	Pos	Dis	In	Tournament	Match	Country	Year	Venue
3	6	lbw	1	L B&H WS	9 v WI	in Aus	1991/92	at Brisbane
46	3	stumped	1	L Tex. Trop	3 v Eng	in Eng	1996	at Manchester
16	3	caught	1	L Singer WS	2 v SL	in SL	1996	at Colombo (RPS) (d/n)
36	3	caught	2	W Singer WS	4 v Zim	in SL	1996	at Colombo (SSC)
59	7	lbw	1	L Singer WS	6 v Aus	in SL	1996	at Colombo (SSC)
DNB	- -		2	W Sahara C.	1 v Pak	in Can	1996	at Toronto
11*	8	not out	1	L Sahara C.	2 v Pak	in Can	1996	at Toronto
12	6	lbw	2	L Sahara C.	5 v Pak	in Can	1996	at Toronto
31	5	caught	2	L Titan Cup	1 v SA	in Ind	1996/97	at Hyderabad(Dec)(d/n)
4	5	run out	2	W Titan Cup	3 v Aus	in Ind	1996/97	at Bangalore (d/n)
54	1	bowled	2	L Titan Cup	4 v SA	in Ind	1996/97	at Jaipur
40	1	caught	2	L Std Bank	1 v SA	in SA	1996/97	at Bloemfontein (d/n)
38	2	caught	2	T Std Bank	3 v Zim	in SA	1996/97	at Paarl (d/n)
0	1	run out	1	L Std Bank	6 v SA	in SA	1996/97	at Port Elizabeth
83	1	run out	1	L Std Bank	7 v SA	in SA	1996/97	at East London (d/n)
31	1	caught	1	L Std Bank	8 v Zim	in SA	1996/97	at Centurion (d/n)
12	1	caught	2	W Std Bank	9 v Zim	in SA	1996/97	at Benoni
18	1	run out	1	N Std Bank	F v SA	in SA	1996/97	at Durban (d/n)
5	1	caught	2	L Std Bank	F v SA	in SA	1996/97	at Durban (d/n)
2	3	run out	1	L 1st ODI	v Zim	in Zim	1996/97	at Bulawayo
39*	2	not out	2	W 2nd ODI	v WI	in WI	1996/97	at Port of Spain
79	2	caught	2	L 3rd ODI	v WI	in WI	1996/97	at Kingstown
4	2	bowled	1	L 4th ODI	v WI	in WI	1996/97	at Bridgetown
62	1	caught wk	2	W Indep Cup	3 v NZ	in Ind	1997	at Bangalore (d/n)
0	1	bowled	1	L Indep Cup	4 v SL	in Ind	1997	at Mumbai (d/n)
33	2	caught	2	L Indep Cup	6 v Pak	in Ind	1997	at Chennai (d/n)
11	2	caught	1	L Asia Cup	3 v SL	in SL	1997	at Colombo (RPS)
TDNB	-		-	N Asia Cup	4 v Pak	in SL	1997	at Colombo (SSC)
73*	1	not out	2	W Asia Cup	6 v BD	in SL	1997	at Colombo (SSC)
34	1	caught	1	L Asia Cup	F v SL	in SL	1997	at Colombo (RPS)
31	2	run out	2	L 1st ODI	v SL	in SL	1997	at Colombo (RPS) (d/n)
113	2	caught	1	L 2nd ODI	v SL	in SL	1997	at Colombo (RPS) (d/n)

14	1	caught	1	N 3rd ODI	v SL	in SL	1997	at Colombo (SSC)
17	2	caught	2	L 3rd ODI	v SL	in SL	1997	at Colombo (SSC)
17	2	caught	1	W Sahara C.	1 v Pak	in Can	1997	at Toronto
32	1	caught	2	W Sahara C.	2 v Pak	in Can	1997	at Toronto
TDNB	-		-	N Sahara C.	3 v Pak	in Can	1997	at Toronto
2	1	caught	1	W Sahara C.	3 v Pak	in Can	1997	at Toronto
75*	2	not out	2	W Sahara C.	4 v Pak	in Can	1997	at Toronto
96	2	caught	1	L Sahara C.	5 v Pak	in Can	1997	at Toronto
0	2	caught	1	L 1st ODI	v Pak	in Pak	1997/98	at Hyderabad (Sind)
2	2	caught	2	W 2nd ODI	v Pak	in Pak	1997/98	at Karachi
26	2	caught	1	L 3rd ODI	v Pak	in Pak	1997/98	at Lahore (d/n)
29	2	bowled	2	L ChT (UAE)	1 v Eng	in UAE	1997/98	at Sharjah (d/n)
90	2	bowled	1	L ChT (UAE)	4 v Pak	in UAE	1997/98	at Sharjah (d/n)
70	1	stumped	2	L ChT (UAE)	6 v WI	in UAE	1997/98	at Sharjah (d/n)
12	1	bowled	2	W 1st ODI	v SL	in Ind	1997/98	at Guwahati
TDNB	-	-	-	N 2nd ODI	v SL	in Ind	1997/98	at Indore
61	2	caught	1	L 3rd ODI	v SL	in Ind	1997/98	at Goa
11	1	caught wk	2	W SJI Cup	1 v BD	in BD	1997/98	at Dhaka
13	1	caught	1	W SJI Cup	2 v Pak	in BD	1997/98	at Dhaka
68	1	lbw	2	W SJI Cup	F1 v Pak	in BD	1997/98	at Dhaka
26	1	caught	1	L SJI Cup	F2 v Pak	in BD	1997/98	at Dhaka
124	1	bowled	2	W SJI Cup	F3 v Pak	in BD	1997/98	at Dhaka
82	1	caught	1	W Pepsi Tri	3 v Zim	in Ind	1997/98	at Vadodara
72	1	caught wk	2	W Pepsi Tri	4 v Aus	in Ind	1997/98	at Kanpur
13	1	caught wk	1	W Pepsi Tri	5 v Zim	in Ind	1997/98	at Cuttack
29	1	caught wk	1	L Pepsi Tri	F v Aus	in Ind	1997/98	at Delhi
105	2	bowled	1	W CCC (UAE)	1v NZ	in UAE	1997/98	at Sharjah (d/n)
8	1	bowled	2	L CCC (UAE)	3 v Aus	in UAE	1997/98	at Sharjah(d/n)
31	2	caught	1	L CCC (UAE)	4 v NZ	in UAE	1997/98	at Sharjah(d/n)
17	1	lbw	2	L CCC (UAE)	6 v Aus	in UAE	1997/98	at Sharjah(d/n)
23	1	caught	2	W CCC (UAE)	F v Aus	in UAE	1997/98	at Sharjah(d/n)
7	1	caught	2	W CC Tri.	1 v BD	in Ind	1998	at Chandigarh (d/n)
9	2	bowled	2	W CC Tri.	3 v Ken	in Ind	1998	at Bangalore (d/n)
36	1	bowled	2	W CC Tri.	F v Ken	in Ind	1998	at Kolkata (d/n)
80	1	caught	2	W Nidahas	1 v SL	in SL	1998	at Colombo (RPS) (d/n)
4	1	caught wk	2	N Nidahas	3 v NZ	in SL	1998	at Colombo (RPS) (d/n)

26	1	caught	2	L Nidahas	7 v SL	in SL	1998	at Colombo (SSC)
TDNB	-	-	-	N Nidahas	8 v NZ	in SL	1998	at Colombo (SSC)
109	1	caught	1	W Nidahas	F v SL	in SL	1998	at Colombo (RPS) (d/n)
54*	1	retire no	2	W Sahara C.	1 v Pak	in Can	1998	at Toronto
23	1	run out	2	L Sahara C.	3 v Pak	in Can	1998	at Toronto
10	1	bowled	2	L Sahara C.	4 v Pak	in Can	1998	at Toronto
9	1	caught	1	L Sahara C.	5 v Pak	in Can	1998	at Toronto
11	1	caught wk	2	W 1st ODI	v Zim	in Zim	1998/99	at Bulawayo
107*	2	not out	2	W 2nd ODI	v Zim	in Zim	1998/99	at Bulawayo
40	1	caught wk	2	L 3rd ODI	v Zim	in Zim	1998/99	at Harare
1	1	caught wk	1	W ICC KO	QFv Aus	in BD	1998/99	at Dhaka (d/n)
83	1	stumped	1	L ICC KO	SFv WI	in BD	1998/99	at Dhaka (d/n)
5	1	caught wk	2	W ChT (UAE)	1 v SL	in UAE	1998/99	at Sharjah (d/n)
28	1	stumped	2	W ChT (UAE)	3 v Zim	in UAE	1998/99	at Sharjah (d/n)
0	2	run out	1	W ChT (UAE)	4 v SL	in UAE	1998/99	at Sharjah (d/n)
1	1	lbw	2	L ChT (UAE)	6 v Zim	in UAE	1998/99	at Sharjah (d/n)
63*	1	not out	2	W ChT (UAE)	F v Zim	in UAE	1998/99	at Sharjah (d/n)
60	1	caught	1	L 1st ODI	v NZ	in NZ	1998/99	at Taupo (d/n)
38	1	caught wk	2	W 2nd ODI	v NZ	in NZ	1998/99	at Napier (d/n)
0	1	caught	1	N 3rd ODI	v NZ	in NZ	1998/99	at Wellington
50	2	caught wk	2	W 4th ODI	v NZ	in NZ	1998/99	at Auckland
60	1	caught	2	L 5th ODI	v NZ	in NZ	1998/99	at Christchurch (d/n)
130*	1	not out	1	W Pepsi Cup	2 v SL	in Ind	1998/99	at Nagpur
13	1	caught wk	2	L Pepsi Cup	3 v Pak	in Ind	1998/99	at Jaipur
65	2	caught wk	1	W Pepsi Cup	5 v SL	in Ind	1998/99	at Pune
57	1	caught	1	L Pepsi Cup	6 v Pak	in Ind	1998/99	at Chandigarh (d/n)
13	1	caught wk	2	L Pepsi Cup	F v Pak	in Ind	1998/99	at Bangalore (d/n)
26	2	lbw	2	L CCC (UAE)	2 v Pak	in UAE	1998/99	at Sharjah (d/n)
7	2	caught wk	1	W CCC (UAE)	3 v Eng	in UAE	1998/99	at Sharjah (d/n)
2	2	bowled	1	W CCC (UAE)	4 v Eng	in UAE	1998/99	at Sharjah (d/n)
50	2	caught	1	L CCC (UAE)	F v Pak	in UAE	1998/99	at Sharjah (d/n)
97	1	run out	1	L World Cup	2 v SA	in Eng	1999	at Brighton
9	1	caught	2	L World Cup	8 v Zim	in Eng	1999	at Leicester
13	2	lbw	1	W World Cup	15v Ken	in Eng	1999	at Bristol
183	2	caught	1	W World Cup	21v SL	in Eng	1999	at Taunton
40	1	run out	1	W World Cup	25v Eng	in Eng	1999	at Birmingham

8	1	bowled	2	L World Cup	Suv Aus	in Eng	1999	at The Oval
29	2	bowled	1	L World Cup	Suv NZ	in Eng	1999	at Nottingham
10	1	lbw	1	L Aiwa Cup	2 v Aus	in SL	1999	at Galle
9	1	run out	1	L Aiwa Cup	3 v SL	in SL	1999	at Colombo (RPS) (d/n)
8	1	caught	2	L Aiwa Cup	5 v Aus	in SL	1999	at Colombo (SSC)
85	4	caught	1	W Aiwa Cup	6 v SL	in SL	1999	at Colombo (SSC)
6	1	caught	1	W S'pore Ch	2 v Zim	in Sin	1999	at Singapore
32	2	stumped	2*	L S'pore Ch	3 v WI	in Sin	1999	at Singapore
23	4	run out	1	N S'pore Ch	F v WI	in Sin	1999	at Singapore
46	4	caught	1	L S'pore Ch	F v WI	in Sin	1999	at Singapore
54*	4	not out	2*	W DMC Cup	1 v WI	in Can	1999	at Toronto
1	4	caught	2*	L DMC Cup	2 v WI	in Can	1999	at Toronto
34	2	bowled	1*	W DMC Cup	3 v WI	in Can	1999	at Toronto
38	2	caught	2	W LG Cup	2 v SA	in Ken	1999/00	at Nairobi (Gym)
21	2	caught	1	W LG Cup	4 v Ken	in Ken	1999/00	at Nairobi (Gym)
139	2	caught	1	W LG Cup	6 v Zim	in Ken	1999/00	at Nairobi (Gym)
10	2	caught wk	2	L LG Cup	F v SA	in Ken	1999/00	at Nairobi (Gym)
41	1	caught	2	L 1st ODI	v NZ	in Ind	1999/00	at Rajkot
4	1	run out	1	W 2nd ODI	v NZ	in Ind	1999/00	at Hyderabad (Decc)
153*	1		1	W 3rd ODI	v NZ	in Ind	1999/00	at Gwalior
17	1	lbw	2	L 4th ODI	v NZ	in Ind	1999/00	at Guwahati
86	2	stumped	2	W 5th ODI	v NZ	in Ind	1999/00	at Delhi
61	2	bowled	1	L C&U Ser.	2 v Pak	in Aus	1999/00	at Brisbane (d/n)
100	2	run out	2	L C&U Ser.	3 v Aus	in Aus	1999/00	at Melbourne (d/n)
5	1	caught wk	1	L C&U Ser.	4 v Aus	in Aus	1999/00	at Sydney (d/n)
43	2	caught	2	L C&U Ser.	7 v Pak	in Aus	1999/00	at Hobart
141	2	lbw	1	W C&U Ser.	9 v Pak	in Aus	1999/00	at Adelaide (d/n)
5	2	caught	2	L C&U Ser.	10v Aus	in Aus	1999/00	at Adelaide (d/n)
1	2	caught wk	2	L C&U Ser.	11v Pak	in Aus	1999/00	at Perth (d/n)
31	1	caught wk	2*	W 1st ODI	v SA	in Ind	1999/00	at Kochi
105*	1	not out	2*	W 2nd ODI	v SA	in Ind	1999/00	at Jamshedpur
56	1	caught wk	1*	L 3rd ODI	v SA	in Ind	1999/00	at Faridabad
87	1	caught	2*	W 4th ODI	v SA	in Ind	1999/00	at Vadodara
6	1	caught	2*	L 5th ODI	v SA	in Ind	1999/00	at Nagpur
27	1	caught	1*	L CCC (UAE)	1 v SA	in UAE	1999/00	at Sharjah (d/n)
25	1	caught wk	2*	W CCC (UAE)	2 v Pak	in UAE	1999/00	at Sharjah (d/n)

7	1	caught	2 *	L CCC (UAE)	4 v Pak	in UAE	1999/00	at Sharjah (d/n)
6	2	caught wk	1 *	L CCC (UAE)	5 v SA	in UAE	1999/00	at Sharjah (d/n)
135*	1	not out	2 *	W Asia Cup	2 v BD	in BD	2000	at Dhaka (d/n)
13	1	caught wk	2 *	L Asia Cup	3 v SL	in BD	2000	at Dhaka (d/n)
8	1	caught	2 *	L Asia Cup	5 v Pak	in BD	2000	at Dhaka (d/n)
66	1	stumped	2 *	W ICC KOPF	v Ken	in Ken	2000/01	at Nairobi (Gym)
24	1	caught wk	1 *	W ICC KO	QF v Aus	in Ken	2000/01	at Nairobi (Gym)
141*	1	not out	1 *	W ICC KO	SF v SA	in Ken	2000/01	at Nairobi (Gym)
117	1	caught	1 *	L ICC KO	F v NZ	in Ken	2000/01	at Nairobi (Gym)
17	1	caught	1 *	L ChT (UAE)	1 v SL	in UAE	2000/01	at Sharjah (d/n)
18	4	caught wk	1 *	W ChT (UAE)	3 v Zim	in UAE	2000/01	at Sharjah (d/n)
66	2	caught	2 *	W ChT (UAE)	5 v Zim	in UAE	2000/01	at Sharjah (d/n)
1	1	caught	2 *	L ChT (UAE)	6 v SL	in UAE	2000/01	at Sharjah (d/n)
3	1	caught	2 *	L ChT (UAE)	F v SL	in UAE	2000/01	at Sharjah (d/n)
44	1	caught	2 *	W 1st ODI	v Zim	in Ind	2000/01	at Cuttack
144	2	caught	1 *	W 2nd ODI	v Zim	in Ind	2000/01	at Ahmedabad
5	1	bowled	1 *	L 3rd ODI	v Zim	in Ind	2000/01	at Jodhpur
71*	1	not out	2 *	W 4th ODI	v Zim	in Ind	2000/01	at Kanpur
6	1	caught	1 *	W 1st ODI	v Aus	in Ind	2000/01	at Bangalore (d/n)
4	1	bowled	1 *	L 2nd ODI	v Aus	in Ind	2000/01	at Pune
0	4	caught	1 *	W 3rd ODI	v Aus	in Ind	2000/01	at Indore
9	1	caught	2 *	L 4th ODI	v Aus	in Ind	2000/01	at Visakhapatnam
74	1	caught	1 *	L 5th ODI	v Aus	in Ind	2000/01	at Goa
2	1	caught wk	2 *	W CCC (Zim)	2 v Zim	in Zim	2001	at Harare
85	1	caught	2 *	W CCC (Zim)	3 v Zim	in Zim	2001	at Bulawayo
20	1	caught wk	2 *	W CCC (Zim)	4 v WI	in Zim	2001	at Bulawayo
62	1	caught	2 *	W CCC (Zim)	6 v WI	in Zim	2001	at Harare
28	1	lbw	2 *	L CCC (Zim)	F v WI	in Zim	2001	at Harare
5	2	caught	2 *	L CCC (SL)	2 v NZ	in SL	2001	at Colombo (RPS) (d/n)
69	5	caught	2 *	L CCC (SL)	3 v SL	in SL	2001	at Colombo (RPS) (d/n)
4	1	lbw	2 *	L CCC (SL)	5 v NZ	in SL	2001	at Colombo (RPS)
0	2	caught	1 *	W CCC (SL)	8 v SL	in SL	2001	at Colombo (SSC)
64	1	caught	2 *	W CCC (SL	9 v NZ	in SL	2001	at Colombo (SSC)
1	1	caught	2 *	L CCC (SL)	F v SL	in SL	2001	at Colombo (RPS) (d/n)
127	1	caught wk	1 *	L Std Bank	1 v SA	in SA	2001/02	at Johannesburg (d/n)
24	1	caught	1 *	W Std Bank	3 v SA	in SA	2001/02	at Centurion (d/n)

DNB	-	-	2 *	W Std Bank	4 v Ken	in SA	2001/02	at Bloemfontein (d/n)
24	1	bowled	2 *	L Std Bank	6 v Ken	in SA	2001/02	at Port Elizabeth d/n)
85	1	caught	2 *	L Std Bank	7 v SA	in SA	2001/02	at East London (d/n)
111	1	caught	1 *	W Std Bank	9 v Ken	in SA	2001/02	at Paarl (d/n)
9	1	caught wk	1 *	L Std Bank	F v SA	in SA	2001/02	at Durban (d/n)
42	1	caught	1 *	W 1st ODI	v Eng	in Ind	2001/02	at Kolkata (d/n)
14	1	caught	2 *	L 2nd ODI	v Eng	in Ind	2001/02	at Cuttack
26	3	bowled	2 *	W 4th ODI	v Eng	in Ind	2001/02	at Kanpur
74	3	caught	2 *	L 5th ODI	v Eng	in Ind	2001/02	at Delhi
80	3	bowled	2 *	L 6th ODI	v Eng	in Ind	2001/02	at Mumbai (d/n)
57	2	stumped	1 *	L 1st ODI	v Zim	in Ind	2001/02	at Faridabad
86	2	run out	1 *	W 2nd ODI	v Zim	in Ind	2001/02	at Chandigarh (d/n)
11	2	bowled	1 *	L 3rd ODI	v Zim	in Ind	2001/02	at Kochi
7	2	caught	2 *	W 4th ODI	v Zim	in Ind	2001/02	at Hyderabad(Dec)(d/n)
28	2	caught wk	1 *	W 5th ODI	v Zim	in Ind	2001/02	at Guwahati
41	1	caught	2 *	W 3rd ODI	v WI	in WI	2001/02	at Bridgetown
39	1	lbw	1 *	L 4th ODI	v WI	in WI	2001/02	at Port of Spain
56	1	caught	1 *	W 5th ODI	v WI	in WI	2001/02	at Port of Spain
43	1	caught	2 *	W NW Series	2 v Eng	in Eng	2002	at Lord's
7	1	lbw	2 *	W NW Series	3 v SL	in Eng	2002	at The Oval
0	1	lbw	1 *	N NW Series	5 v Eng	in Eng	2002	at Chester-le-Street (d/n)
24	2	caught wk	2 *	W NW Series	6 v SL	in Eng	2002	at Birmingham
6	2	caught	2 *	L NW Series	8 v Eng	in Eng	2002	at The Oval
9	1	run out	1 *	W NW Series	9 v SL	in Eng	2002	at Bristol (d/n)
60	2	bowled	2 *	W NW Series	F v Eng	in Eng	2002	at Lord's
13	1	caught	1 *	W ICC KO	3 v Zim	in SL	2002/03	at Colombo (RPS) (d/n)
117*	2	not out	2 *	W ICC KO	11v Eng	in SL	2002/03	at Colombo (RPS) (d/n)
13	2	caught	1 *	W ICC KO	SFv SA	in SL	2002/03	at Colombo (RPS) (d/n)
DNB	-	-	2 *	N ICC KO	F v SL	in SL	2002/03	at Colombo (RPS) (d/n)
DNB	-	-	2 *	N ICC KO	F v SL	in SL	2002/03	at Colombo (RPS) (d/n)
16	2	bowled	1 *	L 1st ODI	v WI	in Ind	2002/03	at Jamshedpur
78	1	caught	1 *	L 2nd ODI	v WI	in Ind	2002/03	at Nagpur
72	1	caught	2 *	W 3rd ODI	v WI	in Ind	2002/03	at Rajkot
28	1	caught wk	2 *	W 4th ODI	v WI	in Ind	2002/03	at Ahmedabad (d/n)
53	1	bowled	1 *	L 5th ODI	v WI	in Ind	2002/03	at Vadodara
14	4	bowled	1 *	L 1st ODI	v NZ	in NZ	2002/03	at Auckland (d/n)
0	1	bowled	2 *	L 2nd ODI	v NZ	in NZ	2002/03	at Napier

4	2	caught wk	1 *	L 3rd ODI	v NZ	in NZ	2002/03	at Christchurch (d/n)
2	5	caught	1 *	L 4th ODI	v NZ	in NZ	2002/03	at Queenstown
0	1	caught wk	2 *	W 5th ODI	v NZ	in NZ	2002/03	at Wellington(WS)(d/n)
23	1	caught wk	2 *	W 6th ODI	v NZ	in NZ	2002/03	at Auckland (d/n)
15	1	bowled	1 *	L 7th ODI	v NZ	in NZ	2002/03	at Hamilton (d/n)
8	1	caught wk	1 *	W World Cup	7 v NL	in SA	2002/03	at Paarl
9	1	caught wk	1 *	L World Cup	11v Aus	in SA	2002/03	at Centurion
24	4	caught	1 *	W World Cup	17v Zim	in Zim	2002/03	at Harare
112*	3	not out	1 *	W World Cup	25v Nam	in SA	2002/03	at Pietermaritzburg
19	3	caught	1 *	W World Cup	30v Eng	in SA	2002/03	at Durban (d/n)
0	3	lbw	2 *	W World Cup	36v Pak	in SA	2002/03	at Centurion
107*	3	not out	2 *	W World Cup	Suv Ken	in SA	2002/03	at Cape Town (d/n)
48	3	bowled	1 *	W World Cup	Suv SL	in SA	2002/03	at Johannesburg
3	3	bowled	2 *	W World Cup	Suv NZ	in SA	2002/03	at Centurion
111*	3	not out	1 *	W World Cup	SFv Ken	in SA	2002/03	at Durban (d/n)
24	3	caught	2 *	L World Cup	F v Aus	in SA	2002/03	at Johannesburg
30	3	caught	1 *	W TVS (BD)	1 v BD	in BD	2003	at Dhaka (d/n)
75	3	caught	1 *	W TVS (BD)	2 v SA	in BD	2003	at Dhaka (d/n)
61	3	caught	1 *	L TVS (BD)	6 v SA	in BD	2003	at Dhaka (d/n)
11*	3	not out	1 *	N TVS (BD)	F v SA	in BD	2003	at Dhaka (d/n)
37	4	caught	2 *	L TVS (Ind)	8 v Aus	in Ind	2003/04	at Bangalore (d/n)
33	3	caught	1 *	W TVS (Ind)	9 v NZ	in Ind	2003/04	at Hyderabad(Decc(d/n)
82	3	run out	2 *	L VB Series	1 v Aus	in Aus	2003/04	at Melbourne (d/n)
32*	5	not out	2 *	W VB Series	3 v Zim	in Aus	2003/04	at Hobart
18	1	caught	1 *	W VB Series	5 v Aus	in Aus	2003/04	at Brisbane (d/n)
33	2	caught	1 *	W VB Series	6 v Zim	in Aus	2003/04	at Brisbane (d/n)
1	1	caught wk	1 *	L VB Series	7 v Aus	in Aus	2003/04	at Sydney (d/n)
1	4	caught	1 *	W VB Series	8 v Zim	in Aus	2003/04	at Adelaide (d/n)
1	5	caught wk	1 *	L VB Series	11v Aus	in Aus	2003/04	at Perth
6	5	caught wk	1 *	L VB Series	F1 v Aus	in Aus	2003/04	at Melbourne (d/n)
3	4	caught	2 *	L VB Series	F2 v Aus	in Aus	2003/04	at Sydney (d/n)
45	3	caught	1 *	W 1st ODI	v Pak	in Pak	2003/04	at Karachi
15	4	stumped	2 *	L 2nd ODI	v Pak	in Pak	2003/04	at Rawalpindi (d/n)
39	5	caught wk	1 *	L 3rd ODI	v Pak	in Pak	2003/04	at Peshawar
21	4	caught wk	2 *	W 4th ODI	v Pak	in Pak	2003/04	at Lahore (d/n)
45	4	caught wk	1 *	W 5th ODI	v Pak	in Pak	2003/04	at Lahore (d/n)

56	3	caught	1 *	W Asia Cup	2 v UAE	in SL	2004	at Dambulla (d/n)
6	4	caught	2 *	L Asia Cup	6 v SL	in SL	2004	at Dambulla (d/n)
60	3	caught	2 *	W Asia Cup	7 v BD	in SL	2004	at Colombo (SSC)
39	3	bowled	2 *	L Asia Cup	10 v Pak	in SL	2004	at Colombo (RPS) (d/n)
79	3	caught	1 *	W Asia Cup	11v SL	in SL	2004	at Colombo (RPS) (d/n)
4	3	caught	2 *	L Asia Cup	F v SL	in SL	2004	at Colombo (RPS) (d/n)
25	2	caught	2 *	L V'con Cup	1 v Pak	in NL	2004	at Amstelveen
TDNB	-	-	*	N V'con Cup	2 v Aus	in NL	2004	at Amstelveen
24	2	caught wk	1 *	L NW Chall.	1 v Eng	in Eng	2004	at Nottingham
7	1	run out	2 *	L NW Chall.	2 v Eng	in Eng	2004	at The Oval
90	1	caught	1 *	W NW Chall.	3 v Eng	in Eng	2004	at Lord's
90	1	bowled	1 *	W ICC KO	3 v Ken	in Eng	2004	at Southampton
0	1	caught wk	1 *	L ICC KO	12v Pak	in Eng	2004	at Birmingham
48	4	caught wk	1 *	L Plat Jub	O v Pak	in Ind	2004/05	at Kolkata (d/n)
0	1	bowled	1 *	W 1st ODI	v BD	in BD	2004/05	at Chittagong (MAA)
22	2	caught	2 *	L 2nd ODI	v BD	in BD	2004/05	at Dhaka (d/n)
55	3	caught	1 *	W 3rd ODI	v BD	in BD	2004/05	at Dhaka (d/n)
22	3	caught	2 *	L Tsunami	O v ICC	in Aus	2004/05	at Melbourne (d/n)
0	3	bowled	1 *	W 1st ODI	v Pak	in Ind	2004/05	at Kochi
9	4	bowled	1 *	W 2nd ODI	v Pak	in Ind	2004/05	at Visakhapatnam
4	4	caught	2 *	L 3rd ODI	v Pak	in Ind	2004/05	at Jamshedpur
18	4	run out	1 *	L 4th ODI	v Pak	in Ind	2004/05	at Ahmedabad
51	2	bowled	1	L IOC Cup	4 v SL	in SL	2005	at Dambulla (d/n)
2*	1	retire no	1	W IOC Cup	6 v WI	in SL	2005	at Colombo (RPS) (d/n)
26	1	lbw	2	L IOC Cup	F v SL	in SL	2005	at Colombo (RPS) (d/n)
5	1	caught wk	2 *	L V'con Tri	2 v NZ	in Zim	2005/06	at Bulawayo
20	1	caught	1 *	W V'con Tri	3 v Zim	in Zim	2005/06	at Harare
19	2	caught	2 *	W V'con Tri	5 v NZ	in Zim	2005/06	at Harare
2	2	caught	2 *	W V'con Tri	6 v Zim	in Zim	2005/06	at Harare
31	2	caught	1 *	L V'con Tri	F v NZ	in Zim	2005/06	at Harare

Career ODIS					
Runs	Pos	Dis	Inn	Vs	Venue
98	2	run out	1	v West Indies	Nagpur
13	1	caught	1	v West Indies	Cuttack
68	2	stumped	1	v West Indies	Vadodara
TDNB	-	-	-	v Sri Lanka	Kolkata
62	2	caught	2	v Sri Lanka	Rajkot
48	1	lbw	2	v Sri Lanka	Margao
58*	2	not out	2	v Sri Lanka	Visakhapatnam
66	1	caught	1	v Bangladesh	Port of Spain
89	2	stumped	1	v Bermuda	Port of Spain
7	2	caught	2	v Sri Lanka	Port of Spain
32	3	bowled	1	v Africa XI	Bangalore
88	3	caught	1	v Africa XI	Chennai
73*	1	not out	2	v Ireland	Belfast
13	1	caught	1	v South Africa	Belfast
42	1	caught	2	v South Africa	Belfast
18	1	caught	2	v South Africa	Belfast
2	1	run out	2	v England	Southampton
39	1	caught	1	v England	Bristol
72	1	caught	2	v England	Birmingham
9	1	caught	1	v England	Manchester
59	1	caught	1	v England	Leeds
53	1	caught	2	v England	The Oval
15	1	caught	1	v England	Lord's
DNB	-	-	2	v Australia	Bangalore
41	1	caught	1	v Australia	Chandigarh
0	1	run out	1	v Australia	Vadodara
86	1	caught	2	v Australia	Nagpur
0	1	caught	2	v Australia	Mumbai
39	1	run out	2	v Pakistan	Guwahati
6	1	bowled	1	v Pakistan	Mohali
39	1	bowled	1	v Pakistan	Kanpur
5	1	caught	2	v Pakistan	Gwalior

Career ODIS Summary									
For	Mat	Inn	No	Runs	HS	Ave	100	50	0
Asia XI	3	3	0	142	88	47.33	0	1	0
India	308	297	23	11221	183	40.95	22	71	16
v Africa XI	2	2	0	120	88	60.00	0	1	0
v Australia	35	33	0	774	100	23.45	1	5	3
v Bangladesh	10	10	2	459	135*	57.37	1	4	1
v Bermuda	1	1	0	89	89	89.00	0	1	0
v England	26	26	1	975	117*	39.00	1	7	1
v ICC World XI	1	1	0	22	22	22.00	0	0	0
v Ireland	1	1	1	73	73*	-	0	1	0
v Kenya	11	10	2	588	111*	73.50	3	2	0
v Namibia	1	1	1	112	112*	-	1	0	0
v Netherlands	1	1	0	8	8	8.00	0	0	0
v New Zealand	32	31	1	1079	153*	35.96	3	6	3
v Pakistan	53	50	3	1652	141	35.14	2	9	4
v South Africa	29	29	3	1313	141*	50.50	3	8	1
v Sri Lanka	44	40	2	1534	183	40.36	4	9	3
v U.A.E.	1	1	0	56	56	56.00	0	1	0
v West Indies	27	27	3	1142	98	47.58	0	11	0
v Zimbabwe	36	36	4	1367	144	42.71	3	7	0
in Australia	18	18	1	558	141	32.82	2	2	0
in Bangladesh	17	17	2	736	135*	49.06	2	5	
in Canada	16	14	4	430	96	43.00	0	4	0
in England	27	27	0	1034	183	38.29	1	7	2
in India	80	77	5	3230	153*	44.86	4	25	5
in Ireland	4	4	1	146	73*	48.66	0	1	0
in Kenya	8	8	1	556	141*	79.42	3	1	0
in Netherlands	2	1	0	25	25	25.00	0	0	0
in New Zealand	12	12	0	266	60	22.16	0	3	3
in Pakistan	8	8	0	280	89	35.00	0	1	1
in Singapore	4	4	0	107	46	26.75	0	0	0
in South Africa	25	24	3	1048	127	49.90	5	2	2
in Sri Lanka	40	36	3	1344	117*	40.72	3	10	1
in U.A.E.	26	26	1	725	105	29.00	1	5	1
in West Indies	9	9	1	420	89	52.50	0	4	0

in Zimbabwe	15	15	1	458	107*	32.71	1	2	0
in Africa	48	47	5	2062	141*	49.09	9	5	2
in Americas	25	23	5	850	96	47.22	0	8	0
in Asia	175	168	11	6422	153*	40.90	10	46	9
in Europe	33	32	1	1205	183	38.87	1	8	2
in Oceania	30	30	1	824	141	28.41	2	5	3
home	78	75	5	3110	153*	44.42	4	24	5
away	100	98	4	3468	135*	36.89	6	23	8
neutral	133	127	14	4785	183	42.34	12	25	3
is captain	147	143	11	5104	144	38.66	11	30	9
is not captain	164	157	12	6259	183	43.16	11	42	7
1st innings	152	152	8	6132	183	42.58	15	35	12
2nd innings	153	148	15	5231	135*	39.33	7	37	4
day only matches	177	171	16	6847	183	44.17	11	47	11
day/night matches	134	129	7	4516	141	37.01	11	25	5
1st position	160	160	11	5671	153*	38.06	10	37	10
2nd position	76	76	5	3475	183	48.94	9	21	3
3rd position	32	32	4	1476	112*	52.71	3	10	2
4th position	20	20	1	472	85	24.84	0	2	1
5th position	8	8	1	184	69	26.28	0	1	0
6th position	2	2	0	15	12	7.50	0	0	0
7th position	1	1	0	59	59	59.00	0	1	0
8th position	1	1	1	11	11*	-	0	0	0
won match	149	147	21	6938	183	55.06	18	41	8
lost match	145	145	1	4317	127	29.97	4	31	6
tied match	1	1	0	38	38	38.00	0	0	0
no result	16	7	1	70	23	11.66	0	0	2
World Cup	21	21	3	1006	183	77.50	4	3	1
Asia Cup	13	12	2	518	135*	74.00	1	4	0
Aus Tri Series (CB)	17	17	1	536	141	77.12	2	2	0
ICC Champions Trophy	13	11	2	665	141*	83.12	3	3	1
tournament finals	31	29	2	1000	124	69.20	3	4	0

Man of the Matches / Series								
Match	Vs	Venue	Season	Runs	Bowling	Catches	Result	Award
Standard Bank International One-Day Series	SA	East London	1996/97	83	DNB	0	won	MoM
Pepsi Asia Cup	BD	Colombo (SSC)	1997	73*	0/24	1	won	MoM
Sahara 'Friendship' Cup (2nd ODI)	Pak	Toronto	1997	32	2/16	1	won	MoM
Sahara 'Friendship' Cup (3rd ODI)	Pak	Toronto	1997	2	5/16	1	won	MoM
Sahara 'Friendship' Cup (4th ODI)	Pak	Toronto	1997	75*	2/29	0	won	MoM
Sahara 'Friendship' Cup (5th ODI)	Pak	Toronto	1997	96	2/33	0	won	MoM
Sahara 'Friendship' Cup	Pak	Canada	1997	222 (55.50)	15/160 (10.66)	3	India	MoS
2nd ODI	Pak	Karachi	1997/98	89	0/39	0	won	MoM
Silver Jubilee Independence Cup (3rd Final)	Pak	Dhaka	1997/98	124	0/5	0	won	MoM
Singer-Akai Nidahas Trophy (1st Match) (d/n)	SL	Colombo (RPS)	1998	80	DNB	0	won	MoM
Sahara 'Friendship' Cup (1st ODI)	Pak	Toronto	1998	54*	3/33	0	won	MoM
2nd ODI	Zim	Bulawayo	1998/99	107*	DNB	1	won	MoM
Pepsi Cup (2nd Match)	SL	Nagpur	1998/99	130*	4/ 21	0	won	MoM
Pepsi Cup	Pak/ SL	India	1998/99	278 (69.50)	6/101 (16.83)	2	Pak	MoS

ICC World Cup (21st Match)	SL	Taunton	1999	183	0/37	0	won	MoM
ICC World Cup (25th Match)	Eng	Birmingham	1999	40	3/27	0	won	MoM
DMC Cup (1st ODI)	WI	Toronto	1999	54*	DNB	0	won	MoM
DMC Cup	WI	Canada	1999	89 (44.50)	3/53 (17.66)	1	Ind	MoS
LG Cup (6th Match)	Zim	Nairobi (Gym)	1999/00	139	DNB	0	won	MoM
3rd ODI	NZ	Gwalior	1999/00	153*	1/33	0	won	MoM
5th ODI	NZ	Delhi	1999/00	86	1/29	0	won	MoM
New Zealand in India	NZ	India	1999/00	301 (75.25)	2/95 (47.50)	1	Ind	MoS
Carlton & United Series (9th Match) (d/n)	Pak	Adelaide	1999/00	141	DNB	0	won	MoM
2nd ODI	SA	Jamshedpur	1999/00	105*	DNB	1	won	MoM
Asia Cup (2nd Match) (d/n)	BD	Dhaka	2000	135*	0/35	0	won	MoM
ICC KnockOut (2nd SF)	SA	Nairobi (Gym),	2000/01	141*	1/5	1	won	MoM
2nd ODI	Zim	Ahmedabad	2000/01	144	DNB	0	won	MoM
4th ODI	Zim	Kanpur	2000/01	71*	5/34	0	won	MoM
Zimbabwe in India	Zim	India	2000/01	264 (88.00)	5/51 (10.20)	0	Ind	MoS
Standard Bank Triangular Tournament (7th Match) (d/n)	SA	East London	2001/02	85	DNB	1	won	MoM
2nd ODI (d/n)	Zim	Chandigarh	2001/02	86	DNB	0	won	MoM
India in West Indies	WI	West Indies	2001/02	136 (45.33)	0/20	2	Ind	MoS
ICC World Cup (2nd Super(d/n)	Ken	Cape Town	2002/03	107*	DNB	0	won	MoM
ICC World Cup (2nd SF) (d/n)	Ken	Durban	2002/03	111*	DNB	0	won	MoM

NatWest Challenge (3rd Match)	Eng	Lord's	2004	90	DNB	0	won	MoM
ICC Champions Trophy (3rd Match)	Ken	Southampton	2004	90	0/21	2	won	MoM
NatWest Series (5th ODI)	Eng	Leeds	2007	59	2/26	0	won	MoM
Sri Lanka	India		2006/07	168 (84.00)	1/43 (43.00)	2	India	MoS

Career Milestones

Tot Mat	In	NO	Tot Runs	HS	Ave	100	50	0	Runs	In No	Vs	Year
34	32	3	1011	113	34.86	1	6	2	17	2	SL	1997
56	52	4	2006	124	41.79	2	15	3	72	2	Aus	1997/98
87	82	7	3036	124	40.48	5	20	4	38	2	NZ	1998/99
110	105	8	4000	183	41.23	7	27	5	85	1	SL	1999
131	126	10	5055	183	43.57	11	30	5	141	1	Pak	1999/00
152	147	13	6016	183	44.89	15	34	5	66	2	Zim	2000/01
180	174	14	7088	183	44.30	18	41	7	111	1	Ken	2001/02
208	200	15	8044	183	43.48	19	48	8	78	1	WI	2002/03
236	228	19	9049	183	43.29	22	53	11	82	2	Aus	2003/04
272	263	20	10018	183	41.22	22	60	14	51	1	SL	2005
279	270	21	10123	183	40.65	22	60	14	31	1	NZ	2005/06
298	288	23	11011	183	41.55	22	69	14	72	2	ENG	2007

Test Batting – Career Summary									
For	Mat	Inns	NO	Runs	HS	Ave	100	50	0
v Australia	24	44	4	1403	144	35.07	2	7	2
v Bangladesh	5	6	0	371	100	61.83	1	3	0
v England	12	19	2	983	136	57.82	3	5	2
v New Zealand	8	15	3	563	125	46.91	3	2	1
v Pakistan	12	20	1	902	239	47.47	2	4	0
v South Africa	17	31	3	947	87	33.82	0	7	4
v Sri Lanka	14	24	1	1064	173	46.26	3	4	2
v West Indies	12	16	2	449	75*	32.07	0	2	1
v Zimbabwe	9	13	1	530	136	44.16	2	1	1
in Australia	11	20	0	696	144	34.80	1	4	1
in Bangladesh	5	6	0	371	100	61.83	1	3	0
in England	9	15	1	915	136	65.35	3	5	1
in India	50	84	10	3180	239	42.97	8	13	6
in New Zealand	4	8	1	194	101*	27.71	1	0	0
in Pakistan	3	3	0	148	77	49.33	0	1	0
in South Africa	8	16	2	506	73	36.14	0	4	2
in Sri Lanka	9	17	1	588	147	36.75	1	3	2
in West Indies	9	12	2	400	75*	40.00	0	2	0
in Zimbabwe	5	7	0	214	101	30.57	1	0	1
home	50	84	10	3180	239	42.97	8	13	6
away	63	104	7	4032	147	41.56	8	22	7
is captain	49	75	7	2561	144	37.66	5	13	4
is not captain	64	113	10	4651	239	45.15	11	22	9
1st position	1	1	0	11	11	11.00	0	0	0
3rd position	12	18	2	752	136	47.00	3	2	2
4th position	15	20	2	1188	239	66.00	3	4	0
5th position	66	99	7	3440	144	37.39	6	18	5
6th position	35	47	5	1725	147	41.07	4	11	6
7th position	3	3	1	96	47	48.00	0	0	0
won match	37	58	9	2284	136	46.61	4	14	5
lost match	35	70	1	1653	87	23.95	0	8	6
drawn match	41	60	7	3275	239	61.79	12	13	2

Career Cumulative Test Batting												
Mat	I	NO	Runs	HS	Ave	100	50	0	R	I	Match Vs	Year
1	1	0	131	131	131.00	1	0	0	131	2	2nd Test v Eng	1996
2	2	0	267	136	133.50	2	0	0	136	1	3rd Test v Eng	1996
2	3	0	315	136	105.00	2	0	0	48	3		
3	4	0	381	136	95.25	2	1	0	66	2	Only Test v Aus	1996/97
3	5	1	402	136	100.50	2	1	0	21*	4		
4	6	1	408	136	81.60	2	1	0	6	2	2nd Test v SA	1996/97
4	7	1	408	136	68.00	2	1	1	0	4		
5	8	1	447	136	63.85	2	1	1	39	1	3rd Test v SA	1996/97
5	9	1	488	136	61.00	2	1	1	41	3		
6	10	1	504	136	56.00	2	1	1	16	2	1st Test v SA	1996/97
6	11	1	504	136	50.40	2	1	2	0	4		
7	12	1	527	136	47.90	2	1	2	23	2	2nd Test v SA	1996/97
7	13	1	557	136	46.41	2	1	2	30	4		
8	14	1	630	136	48.46	2	2	2	73	1	3rd Test v SA	1996/97
8	15	1	690	136	49.28	2	3	2	60	3		
9	16	1	732	136	48.80	2	3	2	42	2	1st Test v WI	1996/97
9	16	1	732	136	48.80	2	3	2	-	4		
10	17	1	738	136	46.12	2	3	2	6	2	2nd Test v WI	1996/97
11	18	1	760	136	44.70	2	3	2	22	2	3rd Test v WI	1996/97
11	19	1	768	136	42.66	2	3	2	8	4		
12	19	1	768	136	42.66	2	3	2	-	2	4th Test v WI	1996/97
13	20	1	768	136	40.42	2	3	3	0	1	1st Test v SL	1997
14	21	1	915	147	45.75	3	3	3	147	2	2nd Test v SL	1997
14	22	1	960	147	45.71	3	3	3	45	4		
15	23	1	1069	147	48.59	4	3	3	109	2	1st Test v SL	1997/98
16	24	1	1168	147	50.78	4	4	3	99	1	2nd Test v SL	1997/98
17	25	1	1341	173	55.87	5	4	3	173	1	3rd Test v SL	1997/98
17	26	1	1352	173	54.08	5	4	3	11	3		
18	27	1	1355	173	52.11	5	4	3	3	1	1st Test v Aus	1997/98
18	28	2	1385	173	53.26	5	4	3	30*	3		
19	29	2	1450	173	53.70	5	5	3	65	2	2nd Test v Aus	1997/98
20	30	2	1467	173	52.39	5	5	3	17	1	3rd Test v Aus	1997/98
20	31	2	1483	173	51.13	5	5	3	16	3		
21	32	2	1530	173	51.00	5	5	3	47	2	Only Test v Zim	1998/99
21	33	2	1566	173	50.51	5	5	3	36	4		
22	34	2	1571	173	49.09	5	5	3	5	1	2nd Test v NZ	1998/99
22	35	2	1619	173	49.06	5	5	3	48	3		
23	36	2	1630	173	47.94	5	5	3	11	2	3rd Test v NZ	1998/99
23	37	3	1731	173	50.91	6	5	3	101*	4		
24	38	3	1785	173	51.00	6	6	3	54	2	1st Test v Pak	1998/99
24	39	3	1787	173	49.63	6	6	3	2	4		
25	40	3	1800	173	48.64	6	6	3	13	1	2nd Test v Pak	1998/99

25	41	4	1862	173	50.32	6	7	3	62*	3		
26	42	4	1879	173	49.44	6	7	3	17	2	1st Match v Pak	1998/99
26	43	4	1903	173	48.79	6	7	3	24	4		
27	44	4	1959	173	48.97	6	8	3	56	1	2nd Match v SL	1998/99
27	45	4	2037	173	49.68	6	9	3	78	3		
28	46	4	2039	173	48.54	6	9	3	2	1	1st Test v NZ	1999/00
28	47	5	2103	173	50.07	6	10	3	64*	3		
29	48	5	2103	173	48.90	6	10	4	0	2	2nd Test v NZ	1999/00
29	48	5	2103	173	48.90	6	10	4	-	4		
30	49	5	2228	173	50.63	7	10	4	125	1	3rd Test v NZ	1999/00
30	50	5	2281	173	50.68	7	11	4	53	3		
31	51	5	2341	173	50.89	7	12	4	60	2	1st Test v Aus	1999/00
31	52	5	2384	173	50.72	7	12	4	43	4		
32	53	5	2415	173	50.31	7	12	4	31	2	2nd Test v Aus	1999/00
32	54	5	2432	173	49.63	7	12	4	17	4		
33	55	5	2433	173	48.66	7	12	4	1	1	3rd Test v Aus	1999/00
33	56	5	2458	173	48.19	7	12	4	25	3		
34	57	5	2460	173	47.30	7	12	4	2	1	1st Test v SA	1999/00
34	58	5	2491	173	47.00	7	12	4	31	3		
35	59	5	2492	173	46.14	7	12	4	1	1	2nd Test v SA	1999/00
35	60	5	2505	173	45.54	7	12	4	13	3		
36	61	5	2589	173	46.23	7	13	4	84	2	Only Test v BD	2000/01
36	61	5	2589	173	46.23	7	13	4	-	4		
37	62	5	2616	173	45.89	7	13	4	27	2	1st Test v Zim	2000/01
37	63	6	2681	173	47.03	7	14	4	65*	4		
38	64	6	2711	173	46.74	7	14	4	30	1	2nd Test v Zim	2000/01
39	65	6	2719	173	46.08	7	14	4	8	1	1st Test v Aus	2000/01
39	66	6	2720	173	45.33	7	14	4	1	3		
40	67	6	2743	173	44.96	7	14	4	23	2	2nd Test v Aus	2000/01
40	68	6	2791	173	45.01	7	14	4	48	3		
41	69	6	2813	173	44.65	7	14	4	22	2	3rd Test v Aus	2000/01
41	70	6	2817	173	44.01	7	14	4	4	4		
42	71	6	2822	173	43.41	7	14	4	5	2	1st Test v Zim	2001
42	71	6	2822	173	43.41	7	14	4	-	4		
43	72	6	2831	173	42.89	7	14	4	9	1	2nd Test v Zim	2001
43	73	6	2831	173	42.25	7	14	5	0	3		
44	74	6	2846	173	41.85	7	14	5	15	1	1st Test v SL	2001
44	75	6	2850	173	41.30	7	14	5	4	3		
45	76	6	2868	173	40.97	7	14	5	18	2	2nd Test v SL	2001
45	77	7	2966	173	42.37	7	15	5	98*	4		
46	78	7	2967	173	41.78	7	15	5	1	1	3rd Test v SL	2001
46	79	7	2997	173	41.62	7	15	5	0	3		
47	80	7	3011	173	41.24	7	15	5	14	1	1st Test v SA	2001/02
47	81	7	3041	173	41.09	7	15	5	30	3		

48	82	7	3083	173	41.10	7	15	5	42	2	2nd Test v SA	2001/02
48	83	8	3087	173	41.16	7	15	5	4*	4		
49	84	8	3134	173	41.23	7	15	5	47	2	1st Test vEng	2001/02
49	84	8	3134	173	41.23	7	15	5	-	4		
50	85	8	3139	173	40.76	7	15	5	5	2	2nd Test v Eng	2001/02
50	86	9	3155	173	40.97	7	15	5	16*	4		
51	87	9	3155	173	40.44	7	15	6	0	2	3rd Test v Eng	2001/02
52	88	9	3193	173	40.41	7	15	6	38	2	1st Test v Zim	2001/02
53	89	9	3329	173	41.61	8	15	6	136	2	2nd Test v Zim	2001/02
53	90	9	3349	173	41.34	8	15	6	20	4		
54	91	9	3354	173	40.90	8	15	6	5	2	1st Test v WI	2001/02
55	92	9	3379	173	40.71	8	15	6	25	1	2nd Test v WI	2001/02
55	93	10	3454	173	41.61	8	16	6	75*	3		
56	94	10	3502	173	41.69	8	16	6	48	1	3rd Test v WI	2001/02
56	95	11	3562	173	42.40	8	17	6	60*	3		
57	96	11	3607	173	42.43	8	17	6	45	1	4th Test v WI	2001/02
58	97	11	3643	173	42.36	8	17	6	36	2	5th Test v WI	2001/02
58	98	11	3671	173	42.19	8	17	6	28	4		
59	99	11	3676	173	41.77	8	17	6	5	2	1st Test v Eng	2002
59	100	11	3676	173	41.30	8	17	7	0	4		
60	101	11	3744	173	41.60	8	18	7	68	1	2nd Test v Eng	2002
60	102	11	3843	173	42.23	8	19	7	99	3		
61	103	11	3971	173	43.16	9	19	7	128	1	3rd Test v Eng	2002
62	104	11	4022	173	43.24	9	20	7	51	2	4th Test v Eng	2002
63	105	11	4026	173	42.82	9	20	7	4	1	1st Test v WI	2002/03
64	106	11	4026	173	42.37	9	20	8	0	2	2nd Test v WI	2002/03
64	106	11	4026	173	42.37	9	20	8	-	4		
65	107	11	4055	173	42.23	9	20	8	29	1	3rd Test v WI	2002/03
65	108	11	4071	173	41.96	9	20	8	16	3		
66	109	11	4088	173	41.71	9	20	8	17	1	1st Test v NZ	2002/03
66	110	11	4090	173	41.31	9	20	8	2	3		
67	111	11	4095	173	40.95	9	20	8	5	1	2nd Test v NZ	2002/03
67	112	11	4100	173	40.59	9	20	8	5	3		
68	113	12	4200	173	41.58	10	20	8	100*	1	1st Test v NZ	2003/04
68	114	12	4225	173	41.42	10	20	8	25	3		
69	115	12	4369	173	42.41	11	20	8	144	2	1st Test v Aus	2003/04
69	115	12	4369	173	42.41	11	20	8	-	4		
70	116	12	4371	173	42.02	11	20	8	2	2	2nd Test v Aus	2003/04
70	117	12	4383	173	41.74	11	20	8	12	4		
71	118	12	4420	173	41.69	11	20	8	37	1	3rd Test v Aus	2003/04
71	119	12	4493	173	41.99	11	21	8	73	3		
72	120	12	4509	173	41.75	11	21	8	16	1	4th Test v Aus	2003/04
72	120	12	4509	173	41.75	11	21	8	-	3		
73	121	12	4586	173	42.07	11	22	8	77	2	3rd Test v Pak	2003/04

74	122	12	4631	173	42.10	11	22	8	45	2	1st Test v Aus	2004/05
74	123	12	4636	173	41.76	11	22	8	5	4		
75	124	12	4645	173	41.47	11	22	8	9	2	2nd Test v Aus	2004/05
75	124	12	4645	173	41.47	11	22	8	-	4		
76	125	12	4702	173	41.61	11	23	8	57	2	1st Test v SA	2004/05
77	126	12	4742	173	41.59	11	23	8	40	2	2nd Test v SA	2004/05
77	126	12	4742	173	41.59	11	23	8	-	4		
78	127	12	4813	173	41.85	11	24	8	71	2	1st Test v BD	2004/05
79	128	12	4901	173	42.25	11	25	8	88	1	2nd Test v BD	2004/05
80	129	12	4922	173	42.06	11	25	8	21	2	1st Test v Pak	2004/05
80	129	12	4922	173	42.06	11	25	8	-	4		
81	130	12	4934	173	41.81	11	25	8	12	1	2nd Test v Pak	2004/05
81	131	12	4946	173	41.56	11	25	8	12	3		
82	132	12	4947	173	41.22	11	25	8	1	2	3rd Test v Pak	2004/05
82	133	12	4949	173	40.90	11	25	8	2	4		
83	134	12	5050	173	41.39	12	25	8	101	2	1st Test v Zim	2005/06
84	135	12	5066	173	41.18	12	25	8	16	2	2nd Test v Zim	2005/06
84	135	12	5066	173	41.18	12	25	8	-	4		
85	136	12	5071	173	40.89	12	25	8	5	1	1st Test v SL	2005/06
86	137	12	5111	173	40.88	12	25	8	40	1	2nd Test vSL	2005/06
86	138	12	5150	173	40.87	12	25	8	39	3		
87	138	12	5150	173	40.87	12	25	8	-	2	1st Test v Pak	2005/06
88	139	12	5184	173	40.81	12	25	8	34	2	3rd Test v Pak	2005/06
88	140	12	5221	173	40.78	12	25	8	37	4		
89	141	13	5272	173	40.18	12	26	8	51*	1	1st Test v SA	2006/07
89	142	13	5297	173	41.06	12	26	8	25	3		
90	143	13	5297	173	40.74	12	26	9	0	2	2nd Test v SA	2006/07
90	144	13	5323	173	40.63	12	26	9	26	4		
91	145	13	5389	173	40.82	12	27	9	66	1	3rd Test v SA	2006/07
91	146	13	5435	173	40.86	12	27	9	46	3		

Career Cumulative – Test Batting continued											
Mat	Inn	NO	Runs	HS	Avg	100	50	0	Run	Match Vs	Year
92	148	13	5548	173	41.09	13	27	9	100	v Bangladesh	2007
93	149	13	5563	173	40.90	13	27	9	15	v Bangladesh	2007
94	151	13	5637	173	40.84	13	27	9	34	v England	2007
95	153	14	5718	173	41.13	13	28	9	79	v England	2007
96	155	14	5812	173	41.21	13	29	9	37	v England	2007
97	157	14	5868	173	41.03	13	29	9	8	v Pakistan	2007
98	159	14	6016	173	41.48	14	29	9	102	v Pakistan	2007
99	161	14	6346	239	43.17	15	30	9	239	v Pakistan	2007
100	163	14	6429	239	43.14	15	30	9	43	v Australia	2007
101	165	14	6547	239	43.35	15	32	9	67	v Australia	2008
102	167	14	6556	239	42.84	15	32	10	9	v Australia	2008
103	169	14	6581	239	42.45	15	32	10	7	v Australia	2008
104	170	14	6605	239	42.33	15	32	10	24	v South Africa	2008
105	172	14	6692	239	42.35	15	33	11	0	v South Africa	2008
106	174	15	6792	239	42.71	15	34	11	87	v South Africa	2008
107	176	15	6819	239	42.35	15	34	11	23	v Sri Lanka	2008
108	178	15	6835	239	41.93	15	34	12	0	v Sri Lanka	2008
109	180	15	6888	239	41.74	15	34	12	35	v Sri Lanka	2008
110	182	16	6961	239	41.93	15	34	12	47	v Australia	2008
111	184	16	7090	239	42.20	16	34	12	102	v Australia	2008
112	186	17	7127	239	42.17	16	34	12	5	v Australia	2008
113	188	17	7212	239	42.17	16	35	13	85	v Australia	2008

Career Milestones—Tests											
Tot Mat	I	NO	Tot Runs	HS	Ave	100	50	0	R	Vs	Year
15	23	1	1069	147	48.59	4	3	3	109	SL	1997/98
27	45	4	2037	173	49.68	6	9	3	78	SL	1998/99
47	80	7	3011	173	41.24	7	15	5	14	SA	2001/02
62	104	11	4022	173	43.24	9	20	7	51	Eng	2002
83	134	12	5050	173	41.39	12	25	8	101	Zim	2005/06
98	159	14	6016	173	41.48	14	29	9	100	Pakistan	2007
111	184	16	7090	239	42.20	16	34	12	102	Australia	2008

Career Milestones—Bowling										
	Mat	In	O	Mdns	Runs	Wkts	BBI	BBM	Ave	5 W/I
Tests	113	99	519.3	110	1681	32	3/28	3/37	52.53	0
ODIs	311	171	760.1	30	3849	100	5/16	5/16	38.49	2

Compiled by: Kashinath Bhattacharjee